Ukrainian Armies 1914–55

P Abbott & E Pinak • Illustrated by O Rudenko & D Adamenko

Series editor Martin Windrow

First published in Great Britain in 2004 by Osprey Publishing
Elms Court, Chapel Way, Botley, Oxford OX2 9LP, United Kingdom
Email: info@ospreypublishing.com

CIP data for this publication is available from the British Library

ISBN 1 84176 668 2

Editor: Martin Windrow
Design: Alan Hamp
Index by Glyn Sutcliffe
Originated by Grasmere Digital Imaging Ltd, Leeds, UK

04 05 06 07 08   10 9 8 7 6 5 4 3 2 1

Printed in China through World Print Ltd.

FOR A CATALOGUE OF ALL BOOKS PUBLISHED BY
OSPREY MILITARY AND AVIATION PLEASE CONTACT:

The Marketing Manager, Osprey Direct UK
PO Box 140, Wellingborough, Northants, NN8 2FA, United Kingdom
Email: info@ospreydirect.co.uk

The Marketing Manager, Osprey Direct USA, c/o MBI Publishing
729 Prospect Avenue, Osceola, WI 54020, USA
Email: info@ospreydirectusa.com

www.ospreypublishing.com

Authors' Note

Spelling: Ukrainian is written in Cyrillic, and transliteration can only be approximate. For instance, the initial letters in *Heneral*, *Haidamak* or *Halychyna* can be rendered as either 'H' or 'G': we have opted for the former. The spellings we have used for cities such as Kyiv (Kiev), Lviv (Lwov) and Odesa (Odessa), and for the Dnipro (Dnieper) river, are the modern Ukrainian forms. The English equivalents given for Ukrainian rank titles are necessarily approximate.

Sources: Most of the information in this book comes from Ukrainian language sources, particularly archival material such as army orders and dress regulations. The best general English-language source for military operations and organization is *Ukraine: A Concise Encyclopaedia* (2 vols), edited by Volodomyr Kubijovich and published by the University of Toronto Press (1963). The two memoirs cited in the text are Paustovsky, K., *In That Dawn,* Harville Press (London 1977); and Shandruk, P., *Arms of Valor,* Robert Speller & Sons (New York 1959).

Acknowledgements

Peter Abbott would like to thank Professor W.Shayan of the Shevchenko Library and Museum in London, and Doctor S.M.Fostun of the Association of Ukrainian Former Combatants in Great Britain, for the help they gave him when he first began to study this subject in the late 1960s. Also Susan Abbott (for assistance with the photographs and many other things), Michael Prevezer, Marcel Roubiçek, Osprey co-author Nigel Thomas, and order-of-battle guru Mike Cox, who was instrumental in bringing himself and Eugen Pinak together.
Eugene Pinak would like to thank his father Roman and his mother Tatiana for their support during this undertaking. Also Sergij Muzichuk of *Ordostrij* ('Uniform') Magazine for his help.

Glossary

USS	Ukrainian Legion in Austro-Hungarian service, 1914
ZUNR	Western Ukrainian People's Republic, 1918–20
UHA	Army of the ZUNR
UNR	(Eastern) Ukrainian People's Republic, 1917–21
UTR	Central *Rada* (government) of the UNR
UkSSR	Ukrainian Socialist Soviet Republic (Bolshevik), 1919–21
OUN	Ukrainian Nationalist Organization in exile (1920s–30s)
DUN	OUN armed units (German-sponsored), 1939–41
UDP, UOP, UPP, UNS, SKV, OPV	Ukrainian police & auxiliary units under German occupation, from 1941
UVV	Ukrainian National Liberation Army (German-sponsored), from 1943
UNA	Ukrainian National Army (German-sponsored), 1945
UPA	Ukrainian Insurgent Army, 1941–55

UKRAINIAN ARMIES 1914-55

HISTORICAL BACKGROUND

T HE UKRAINIANS are the largest of the long-submerged nations of Eastern Europe. They are also one of the least well known to Westerners, few of whom are aware that the 20th century produced three separate, self-governing Ukrainian states before the collapse of the Soviet Union allowed the present one to be established in 1991. More-over, the largest of those (the ex-Russian Ukrainian People's Republic, UNR) was ruled by three very different regimes even between 1917 and 1920; and there were also other armed independence movements, all with their own uniforms and insignia. This brief account is thus intended as an introduction for the Western reader to a very complicated subject.

These earlier 20th century Ukrainian regimes all faced the same problem: a circle of powerful and predatory neighbours, coupled with a lack of defensible frontiers (a fact enshrined in the country's very name, for *Ukraina* simply means 'borderland'). All were ultimately overcome, though not before their armies had performed some heroic deeds in the face of almost insuperable odds.

Captain Vasyl Didushok, Ukrainian *Sich* Rifles or Legion, 1915. His rank stars are arranged in the orthodox Austro-Hungarian fashion, though the Legion usually wore them in a line. The standard collar patch was blue, but some individuals added yellow piping or edging.

Western and Eastern Ukraine

Although the Ukrainians now have their own state, it is essential to bear in mind that they were never brought together under one administration until 1945. Historically, the principal division has always been between west and east. This dates back to the Middle Ages, when the Ukrainian heartland was split between the ancient Duchy of Galicia (*'Halychyna'* in Ukrainian) on the northern flanks of the Carpathian mountains in the west, and the equally ancient Principality of Kyiv (Kiev) on the upper Dnipro (Dnieper) river in the east. Galicia became part of the expanding Polish kingdom. The Kyivan state was the forerunner of modern Russia and its cultural ancestor, but in time it too declined and was gobbled up by its neighbours. At first much of its territory also came under Polish control, but the Russian Empire which arose to the north took its eastern portion and began to encroach upon the rest. When Poland itself came to be partitioned during the 18th century, Austria took Galicia and Russia the remainder of its Ukrainian territories. One aspect of these historical divisions was that the Western Ukrainians tended to belong to the Greek Catholic or Uniate Church, which follows Orthodox rites but acknowledges Papal authority, whereas the Easterners remained Russian Orthodox.

Although most of the Austrian-Hungarian Ukrainians (often called 'Ruthenians') lived in Galicia, some were to be found in neighbouring Bukovyna, while others had crossed the Carpathians and settled in the eastern tip of Slovakia. Galicia and Bukovyna fell within the Austrian half of the Dual Monarchy, but Slovakia came under Hungarian rule. Galicia as a whole had a substantial Polish minority, while the Ukrainians were in a minority in Bukovyna, and within Slovakia as a whole. When the Austro-Hungarian Empire broke up in 1918 these competing ethnic claims led to fighting between the resurgent Poles and the Western Ukrainians for control of Galicia, while Bukovyna fell to Rumania, and Slovakia joined Czechoslovakia.

The territories which became the Russian Ukraine were originally limited to the inland areas on either side of the Dnipro river, which were known as 'Right Bank' (Western) and 'Left Bank' (Eastern) Ukraine, after an early Polish-Russian partition. The open steppes which cut the region off from the Black Sea formed the Southern or Tartar Frontier. This was for long a no-man's land, which led to the growth of a strong, independent Cossack tradition. Like their Russian equivalents, the Ukrainian Cossacks were originally self-governing freebooters, many of them escaped serfs. One famous community was known as the *Zaporizhska Sich* ('*sich*' means 'stronghold'). As a result, terms such as '*Kozak*', '*Zaporozhian*', '*Sich*', '*Otaman*' (a Cossack leader) and '*Haidamak*' (an 18th century peasant rebel) came to embody cherished Ukrainian military traditions, and were revived as military titles during the 20th century, along with the costumes associated with them.

These independent Ukrainian Cossacks were brought under Russian control during the 18th century and disappeared as a separate group, except for a number who were transferred to the Black Sea area and who eventually became the Kuban Cossacks. These continued to speak

Ukrainian territories, 1917–24

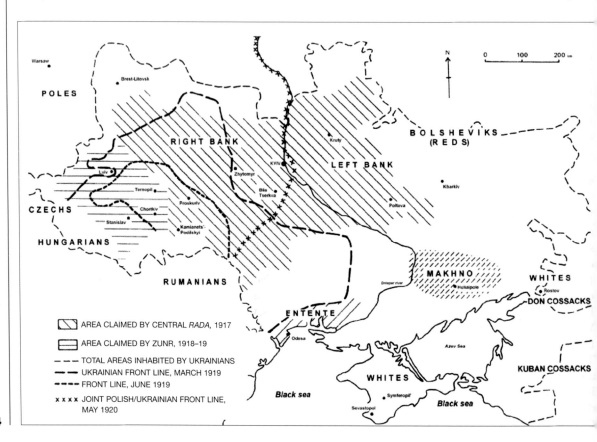

▨	AREA CLAIMED BY CENTRAL *RADA*, 1917
▭	AREA CLAIMED BY ZUNR, 1918–19
– – –	TOTAL AREAS INHABITED BY UKRAINIANS
▬▬	UKRAINIAN FRONT LINE, MARCH 1919
■■■■	FRONT LINE, JUNE 1919
x x x x	JOINT POLISH/UKRAINIAN FRONT LINE, MAY 1920

Ukrainian, but their traditions were different and they played little or no part in the struggle for national independence.

As the Tartars lost control of the grasslands to the south and south-east these were opened up by Ukrainian farmers, who thus extended the Ukrainian-speaking area eastwards across the neck of the Crimean peninsula and into the steppes north of the Sea of Azov. These areas remote from the Ukrainian heartland were less affected by the growth of national consciousness towards the end of the 19th century. The territory over which the ex-Russian Ukrainian People's Republic of 1917–20 exercised effective control lay mostly to the west of Kyiv, and its nationalist message appealed far less to the population further east, whose Ukrainian-speaking peasantry were commonly known as 'Little Russians'.

Overall, the general level of Ukrainian national consciousness at the time of World War I remained lower than among neighbouring groups such as the Czechs or Poles. There were undoubtedly many patriotic idealists who were prepared to fight for an independent Ukraine, but this feeling was strongest among the intelligentsia, together with the population of the Western or Austro-Hungarian Ukraine, and there were many (especially the larger landowners) in the Russian-controlled part who favoured a future within a federation of White Russian states. Others still (particularly the urban proletariat in the industrialized Eastern Ukraine) undoubtedly sympathized with the Bolshevik cause. Finally, a large proportion of the peasants were apathetic or even hostile, wanting only to be left alone, and Anarchist bands (collectively known as 'Greens') were particularly active in Southern and Eastern Ukraine during the Russian Civil War.

Hetman Pavlo Skoropadski (right), who briefly ruled the ex-Russian Eastern Ukraine in 1918, with Kaiser Wilhelm II during a mission to Berlin in that year. Note the Hetman's non-regulation but very popular Caucasian Cossack-style uniform; he holds a small mace, an old symbol of Ukrainian Hetman authority – see Plate C2.

The collapse of the empires, 1917–18

The collapse of the Russian and Austro-Hungarian Empires as a result of World War I gave each part of the Ukrainian heartland the chance to assert its independence. Their differing traditions led them to create two separate states: the ex-Russian Ukrainian People's Republic (UNR) with its capital at Kyiv, and the ex-Austrian Western Ukrainian People's Republic (ZUNR) centred on Lviv. These two entities made a tentative attempt to create a federation; but the fact that they had different enemies (the Easterners were menaced by both 'White' and 'Red' Russians, whereas the Westerners found themselves fighting the Poles) created problems. At times each was actually forced to ally itself with its opposite number's foes. The presence of Austro-German occupying troops up to the end of 1918, and the subsequent attempts by the victorious Entente (the Allies) to intervene in what they called 'Southern Russia', added to the chaos – as did the fact that Ukraine became a battleground during both the Russian Civil War (1918–20) and the Russo-Polish War (1919–20).

Armoured cars in the service of the ex-Russian Ukrainian People's Republic (UNR), named 'Otaman Konovalets' and 'Otaman Melnik'. Despite the poor quality it is possible to make out the trident badges painted on both vehicles.

The fighting of those years flowed backwards and forwards, due to Ukraine's lack of defensible frontiers, and the relatively small size of the armies manoeuvring over large territories (Kyiv changed hands 11 times, if one includes coups). The accompanying chronology should help readers to follow events during this extremely complicated period. By 1921 the Ukrainian lands had been partitioned once again, with Poland, Czechoslovakia and Rumania dividing the Western portion, and Soviet Russia taking the remainder. However, nationalist exiles kept the concept of Ukrainian statehood alive and even received a certain amount of discreet encouragement from Russia's enemies, notably Poland.

The dismemberments of World War II

The approach of World War II raised Ukrainian hopes again, not least because Hitler's dismemberment of Czechoslovakia in 1938 allowed the 'Ruthenians' of Carpatho-Ukraine a brief taste of independence (theirs was the third genuinely autonomous Ukrainian state). However, their small country was overrun by the Hungarians in 1939 (the Carpatho-Ukrainians contend with some justice that it was they who fired the first shots of World War II). Even worse, the cynically self-serving Nazi-Soviet Pact which partitioned Poland after the invasions of 1939 awarded Galicia to the USSR, although it had never been part of the Russian Empire, and it was not until 1941 that the Germans finally entered Ukrainian territory.

When they did so they were greeted as liberators, and Ukrainian volunteers flocked to their colours. However, an independent Slav state (no matter how friendly) did not fit Hitler's vision of a subservient *Ostland*, and much of this initial goodwill was wantonly destroyed by the Nazi occupation policy. It was not until the war had clearly been lost that Germany finally and grudgingly recognized Ukrainian 'independence'. By then all the Ukrainian territories had been overrun by Soviet troops; this de-facto annexation was formalized in 1945, although some indomitable Ukrainian guerrillas continued the struggle into the 1950s. Genuine Ukrainian independence had to await the collapse of the Soviet Empire at the beginning of the 1990s.

It must be admitted that the Ukrainian forces were seldom a match for the major contenders for power over their territories, and the 'divisions' and 'corps' described below should not be thought of as resembling contemporary Western formations in terms of numbers, discipline, levels of equipment or even uniformity of dress. Nevertheless, a great many men have fought and died for the blue and yellow Ukrainian flag during the 20th century, and the forces they served in deserve to be better known than they are.

Given their number and variety, it has seemed best to deal with these forces sequentially, describing each's history, organization, equipment, uniforms and insignia in turn. However, those of the World War II period mostly wore German uniforms, albeit with varying kinds of Ukrainian insignia. We have accordingly thought it best to place most of the pictorial emphasis on the earlier uniforms, which are not only less familiar but frequently more picturesque. Hopefully, this book will do something to rescue these 'unknown armies' from their relative oblivion.

WORLD WAR I

Ukrainian units in the Austro-Hungarian Army, 1914–18

There were no wholly Ukrainian units before 1914, though a number of Austrian regiments incorporated Ukrainian-speaking conscripts from Galicia and Bukovyna, and some Hungarian ones included 'Ruthenians' from Carpathia. The Galicians in particular were so loyal to the Hapsburgs that they were called 'Eastern Tyroleans'. However, growing Ukrainian national consciousness had led to the growth of nationalist organizations such as the *Sich* and *Sokil*, which provided secret paramilitary training from 1909 onwards. 1913 saw the formation of *Striltsi* (Rifle) associations along the lines of Pilsudski's Polish Rifle Clubs.

When the Great War broke out in 1914 some 28,000 *Striltsi* volunteered to join a Ukrainian Legion similar to the Polish equivalent.

CHRONOLOGY, 1914–20

1914 **W.Ukraine (Galicia)**
Aug — Ukrainian *Sich* Rifles formed
1917 **ex-Russian Ukraine**
Mar — First Russian Revolution
Nov — Bolshevik Revolution. Central *Rada* in Kyiv proclaims Ukrainian People's Republic (UNR)
Dec — Fighting with Reds begins
1918 **ex-Russian Ukraine**
Jan — Reds proclaim Ukrainian Socialist Soviet Republic
Feb — Reds take Kyiv
Mar — Reds & *Rada* sign Treaty of Brest-Litovsk with Central Powers. Austro-German troops enter Russian Ukraine, occupy Kyiv & restore *Rada*
Apr — *Rada* replaced by Hetmanate
Nov — **W.Ukraine (Galicia)**
Western Ukrainian People's Republic (ZUNR) proclaimed, and its army (UHA) formed. Fighting with Poles begins
ex-Russian Ukraine
Anti-Hetmanate rebels form Directory. Austro-Germans agree to leave Ukraine. Hetman enlists White Russian help
Carpatho-Ukraine
Ruthenian *Rada* divided between pro-Czechs, pro-Hungarians and pro-Ukrainians
Dec — **ex-Russian Ukraine**
Directory forces take Kyiv. Entente troops land at Odesa and clash with Ukrainians
1919 **ex-Russian Ukraine**
Jan — Directory fighting Red & White Russians, Poles, Ukrainians & Entente troops
Carpatho-Ukraine
Czechs, Hungarians & Rumanians all occupy parts of province
Feb — **ex-Russian Ukraine**
Directory agrees armistice with Rumanians & Entente, but Reds take Kyiv
Mar — Entente troops evacuate Odesa
May — **W.Ukraine (Galicia)**
Poles gain advantage. Rumanians occupy Bukovyna
ex-Russian Ukraine
Directory forces confined to pocket around Brody.

Armistice with Poles allows counter-offensive. Directory establishes capital at Kamanets Podil'skyi
Carpatho-Ukraine
Rada opts to join Czechoslovakia
June — **W.Ukraine (Galicia)**
UHA counter-attacks Poles
July — Poles rally, and force UHA out of Galicia. UHA joins Directory forces
ex-Russian Ukraine
Aug — Denikin's Whites drive Reds out of Ukraine. Joint Directory-UHA forces occupy Kyiv & Odesa; but expelled again by Whites.
Sept — Ukrainians squeezed against Poles & Reds by White advance
Oct — **W.Ukraine (Galicia)**
UHA decimated by typhus
ex-Russian Ukraine
Reds stop Denikin's thrust towards Moscow, counter-attack, rout the Whites and retake Kyiv. Directory forces decimated by typhus
Nov — **W.Ukraine (Galicia)**
UHA joins Denikin's Whites
ex-Russian Ukraine
Directory makes peace with Poles once again, and retires behind Polish lines
1920 **W.Ukraine (Galicia)**
Jan — UHA joins Reds
Apr — UHA changes sides once more, joining Polish-Directory forces
ex-Russian Ukraine
Joint Polish-Directory forces push into Ukraine and drive Reds from Kyiv
May — Red counter-offensive drives Polish-Directory forces back
June — Reds retake Kyiv
Oct — **W.Ukraine (Galicia)**
Russo-Polish peace leaves Poland in control of Galicia
ex-Russian Ukraine
Russo-Polish peace leaves Reds in control of former Russian Ukraine. Ukrainian exiles later launch unsuccessful raids from Ukrainian territory now incorporated into Poland.

A sergeant/officer candidate
of the Ukrainian *Sich* Rifles
or Legion in Austro-Hungarian
service, 1917. Note his
Mazepynka kappi headgear,
and the collar stars in line.

However, the Austro-Hungarian authorities initially accepted only 2,500, and most Ukrainian-speakers still had to serve in 'German' or Hungarian regiments.[1] Ukrainians called the volunteers the *Legion Ukrainskikh Sichovykh Srtiltsiv* (USS) or Ukrainian *Sich* Rifles. They were organized into ten companies, and split up into small 20-man platoons for scouting purposes; but losses were high, and the companies were subsequently brought together to form a regiment-sized formation consisting of ten companies (formed into two battalions), one MG company (with four guns), one infantry gun company (two guns and two mortars), one pioneer company, and one cavalry squadron (later expanded to two, though these seem to have been disbanded in 1917). The Legion, attached to the Austro-Hungarian XXV Corps, suffered heavy losses during September 1916 and was reduced to battalion size, but was reorganized and expanded again in 1917.

The pre-war *Sich* **uniforms** were khaki, while the *Sokil*'s were grey. The *Striltsi* wore khaki uniforms with a distinctive '*Mazepynka*' cap having outwards-sloping sides and a 'V'-shaped cut-out at the front. This last (see Plate A1) was a traditional feature of Cossack headgear named after Ivan Mazepa, the Hetman who fought Peter the Great at the start of the 18th century.

The Ukrainian *Sich* Rifles wore the old blue Austrian uniform at first, then the standard pike-grey. After 1915 the colour became field-grey and the tunic received a stand-and-fall collar instead of the previous standing pattern. Puttees appear to have been standard from the start. The *kappi* bore on its left side a blue cloth rosette with a yellow centre. The regulation cockade worn on the front was of the 'German' pattern – a dull brass or iron disc with the cut-out letters 'FJI' since Galicia and Bukovyna were both Austrian provinces, though in some cases it took the form of the lion of Galicia. The collar patch was plain blue[2]; this became a blue and yellow stripe in 1916.

The Austro-Hungarian authorities regarded the Legionaries as 'irregulars', and an order issued in January 1915 required their officers and NCOs to wear the rosettes used by officials rather than the six-pointed rank stars of the regular KuK units. They ignored this, although the stars were worn arranged in line as prescribed for military officials. The stars and lace were of silver and gold respectively.

A modified uniform was adopted in 1917, provided from the Legion's own sources and worn by all ranks. It included a *Mazepynka kappi* and a new tunic based on the *Karlbluse* which Austro-Hungarian officers were starting to wear at this time (see Plate A2). The cap still bore the Imperial cockade (now a plain 'K' for the new Emperor Karl); but the cloth Ukrainian cockade on the side was replaced by a metal version bearing the Galician lion on a hillside inscribed 'YCC 1914' in gold on blue (the Cyrillic letters stood for 'USS'). This cockade took the place of the stencilled unit identification (as a volunteer unit, the Legion remained outside the regular Austro-Hungarian military structure). The rank badges continued to be of Austrian pattern.

Ukrainians in the Russian Army, 1914–17

There were no separate Ukrainian units in the Russian Army before 1914, though Ukrainian-speakers were in a majority in the Ukraine-based units.

---

1 See MAA 392 & 397, *The Austro-Hungarian Forces in World War I (1) 1914–16 & (2) 1916–18.*
2 Plate G4 in MAA 392 is incorrect in this respect.

They also made up most of the Kuban Cossacks and a substantial proportion of the Terek Cossacks. These Hosts had their own separate traditions, however, and were not strongly influenced by the resurgence of Ukrainian national feeling. There were no specifically Ukrainian uniforms or insignia, and standard Russian arms and equipment were carried.[3]

THE STRUGGLE FOR INDEPENDENCE, 1917–21

THE EX-RUSSIAN UKRAINE:
The Central *Rada*, 1917–18

After the collapse of the Tsarist regime in March 1917, Ukrainians serving in Russian units began to come together to form ad hoc Ukrainian units. Originally a spontaneous movement among the troops themselves, this process was subsequently organized by a Ukrainian General Military Committee. It received official sanction in June 1917, when the Provisional Government in Moscow agreed to the formation of such units on condition that this did not destroy the unity of the Russian Army.

The main formations involved were the 1st Ukrainian *Khmelnytsky Kozak* or *Hetman Bohdan Khmelnytsky* Regiment (formed from Ukrainian members of the Kyiv garrison); three *Shevchenko* regiments formed from garrison units in Moscow; the *Hetman Polubotok* Regt from Ukrainian soldiers at Hrushky near Kyiv; two *Doroshenko* regiments in Symferopol and Chernihiv respectively; a mounted regiment in the Hryshyne region; a *Nalyavaiko* Battalion; *Haidamak* garrisons in Odesa and Katerynoslav; a mounted *Hordienko Haidamak* Regt near Myr; the 1st Railway Regt near Kyiv; and the *Haidamatsky Kish Slobidskoi Ukrainy* or Haidamak Host in Kyiv. There was even a small Ukrainian unit in the Far East.

Some Russian formations were 'Ukrainianized', including a number of Army Corps on the Northern, Western, South-Western and Rumanian Fronts; many of these were pre-war formations with depots located in Ukraine. Some were actually renumbered in accordance with a new Ukrainian system: they included the 1st Ukrainian (ex-34th), 2nd *Zaporizhska Sich* (ex-6th), and 3rd Ukrainian (ex-21st) corps.

In March 1917 a provisional Ukrainian government known as the *Ukrainska Tsentralna Rada* or Central *Rada* was formed in Kyiv ('*Rada*' is the Ukrainian equivalent of the Russian 'Soviet' or assembly). This body was nationalist and broadly democratic. After the Bolsheviks' 'October Revolution' (November in the new-style calendar) the *Rada* declared the independence of the *Ukrainska Narodna Respublika* (Ukrainian People's Republic) or UNR, though 'without breaking federal relations with Russia'. At this period Kyiv was still the headquarters of the Russian Army's Kyiv Military District, whose senior officers continued to support Moscow; they were disarmed and expelled. The new state adopted a flag of yellow over light blue (long regarded as the Ukrainian national colours), and chose the *tryzub* (the trident of St Volodymyr the Great, Grand Prince of Kyiv AD 979–1015) as its symbol.

The main units under Central *Rada* control were the 1st Ukrainian and 2nd *Zaporozhian Sich* Corps (the latter including the *Haidamak* Cavalry Regt and a horse artillery regiment). The *Rada* tried to recall all the Ukrainian units serving in non-Ukrainian areas of Russia, but few succeeded in returning, though the *Hordienko Haidamak* Regt managed to fight its way back from Russia's Western Front in January 1918. An attempt was made to form the other returnees into two *Serdiuk* (Guard) Divisions in November 1917. These comprised the *Khmelnytsky, Polubotok, Doroshenko, Bohun* and *Nalyavaiko* regiments, a St George Regt, a cavalry regiment, and artillery and engineer units. However, they were quickly disbanded again.

Russia was still a combatant against the Central Powers at this point, and a French military mission arrived in Kyiv during autumn 1917 to co-ordinate the operations of the various Entente forces then in Ukraine (these included the Czechoslovakian and Polish corps as well as the Ukrainians themselves), in order to help keep Rumania in the conflict. Some of these Entente troops helped the *Rada* to suppress local revolts – at this period the *Rada* was pro-Western.

The *Rada*'s strength lay in a number of volunteer formations, such as the *Pomichnyi Kurin Ukrainskikh Sichovykh Striltsiv* (Auxiliary Battalion of *Sich* Riflemen, recruited largely from Kyiv students), and the *Haidamatskyi Kish Slobidskoi Ukrainy* led by Simon Petliura (this unit had 'Red' and 'Black' *Haidamak* battalions and an artillery battery). In addition, there were a Black Sea Bn, an artillery group (two batteries) and an armoured car unit, reinforced in January by the *Hordienko Haidamak* Regiment. One of the most effective of the *Rada*'s units was the *Galitsko-Bukovinsky Kurin Sichovykh Striltsiv* (Galician-Bukovynian Bn of *Sich* Riflemen), composed of Western Ukrainians captured by the Russians and held in a large POW camp at Kyiv; some had been in the Ukrainian *Sich* Rifles, though most would have served in regular Austro-Hungarian regiments. This well-trained, well-disciplined unit was sometimes known as 'Konovalet's Rifles' after its colonel.

There were also a number of volunteer local defence forces founded in May 1917 and known as the *Vilne Kozatstvo* or Free Cossacks. Such units were first formed in Right Bank Ukraine and subsequently spread to the Poltava region and most of the Left Bank. Their organization was based on village companies (of 35 to 70 men), which were loosely organized into county battalions, district regiments and provincial brigades. Their officers were elected.

The *Rada*'s attempt to recall the Russian Army's Ukrainian units quickly led to a break with the new Bolshevik government in Moscow. Fighting broke out in December 1917, and most of the existing regular Ukrainian forces quickly fell apart. The main resistance to the advancing Reds was put up by the various volunteer units, and 16 small Free Cossack battalions formed from the Kyiv workers. The Entente's Polish formations in Ukraine also tried to resist the Bolshevik advance, but had to retreat, and Kyiv was lost to the Reds early in February 1918. The Central *Rada* had a doctrinaire preference for a militia-style popular army, which led to the formal disbandment of the remaining regular units in January 1918. It tried to turn the Free Cossacks into a territorial militia by establishing village quotas and creating instructional units (one infantry and one cavalry company per county), but in practice they remained largely localized and independent.

The 'Greycoat' Division, formed from prisoners in Austro-Hungarian camps, being inspected by Austro-Hungarian officers just before their transfer to Ukrainian command in 1918. The 'Greycoat' officers are wearing their insignia directly on the collar with a blue-yellow stripe behind. Later they placed them on Ukrainian patches.

These measures were unsuccessful, and the *Rada* had to approach the Central Powers for help; the latter, hungry for Ukraine's crops and other economic resources, were happy to insist that the Bolsheviks recognize Ukraine's independence as one the terms of the Treaty of Brest-Litovsk in March 1918. The new state promptly became an Austro-German satellite, and some 35 German and Austro-Hungarian divisions moved in, the latter's contingent including the Ukrainian *Sich* Rifles. The pro-Entente Polish troops in Ukraine were forced to surrender to the Germans, while the Czechs retired eastward and subsequently became the Czechoslovak Legion of Russian Civil War fame.

The local Ukrainian volunteer forces which had survived the early fighting were reorganized to form two larger corps, the *Haidamatskyi Kish Slobidskoi Ukrainy* and *Zaporizhska* Groups. The latter subsequently became a division (absorbing the *Haidamak* Regt), and helped the advancing Austro-German forces to liberate Kyiv again in March 1918. The Galician *Sich* Rifles had also managed to survive as a unit; they served as a guard for the *Rada*, and were expanded to regimental size in March. Many of the new recruits were local volunteers, and the term 'Galician' was accordingly dropped.

By this time the *Rada* had been forced to abandon its militia concept. The Free Cossacks were disbanded in March, and the *Rada* now planned to raise a conscript army of eight provincial corps (Kyiv, Volyn, Podillia, Odesa, Chernihiv, Poltava, Kharkiv and Katerynoslav) and four and a half cavalry divisions; but this project had not progressed far before the regime was overthrown in April 1918. At that stage its army was about 15,000 strong, of whom 2,000 were cavalry, with 60 guns, 250 machine guns and 12 armoured cars.

Meanwhile, the Germans had agreed to form their Ukrainian POWs into *Sinyozhupanna* ('Bluecoat') Divisions. These were supposed to have four infantry and one artillery regiment apiece, but they must have been far understrength, since the two 'divisions' actually formed only numbered 1,200 men each. The 1st began to arrive in Ukraine in April 1918. The Austro-Hungarians were forming a *Sirozhupanna* or 'Greycoat' Division from Ukrainians in their prison camps, also with four infantry regiments and supporting units.

*   *   *

There seems to be no record of any official Ukrainian uniform distinctions being introduced during the 'Ukrainianization' period, but

Four members of the 'Greycoat' Division, 1918: under magnification they can be identified as (left to right) a *Bunchuzhnyi, Chotovyi, Roiovyi* and a *Kozak* – sergeant-major, sergeant, corporal and private.

a number of units adopted unofficial insignia in the national colours. Independence saw more of these appear, including yellow and light blue armbands on the left sleeve, and a cloth rosette with a yellow centre within a blue ring.

For lack of other resources, troops went on wearing the Tsarist Russian uniform. In **December 1917** the *Rada* officially adopted this; the cloth rosette was retained, although the *Sich* Rifles and other Kyiv garrison troops used a non-regulation cockade in the form of a metal shield bearing the winged figure of St Mikhail holding a sword in its right hand and a shield bearing the Galician lion in the other, with a *tryzub* over all: the shield was blue and the devices and edging yellow. Lozenge-shaped blue patches piped with yellow were officially introduced for wear on the collar of the greatcoat only, that of the *gimnastiorka* or blouse being too narrow. Blue shoulder straps piped with yellow were prescribed.

The Russian ranks and insignia were abolished, and the new ranks were functional. The devices consisted of silver braid chevrons worn point upwards on the upper right arm, with the braid having a more elaborate zig-zag pattern for senior officers, as follows: *Otaman Frontu* (Front Commander), 3 broad chevrons with a loop above; *Otaman Armii* (Army Cdr), 2 broad chevrons with a loop; *Otaman Korpusu* (Corps Cdr), 1 broad chevron with a loop; *Otaman Divisii* (Division Cdr), 3 broad chevrons with no loop; *Otaman Brigady* (Brigade Cdr), 2 such chevrons; *Polkovnik* (Regiment Cdr), 1 chevron; *Osavul* (Deputy Regt Cdr), 4 narrow chevrons with a loop; *Kurinnyi* (Battalion Cdr), 3 such chevrons with a loop; *Sotnyk* (Company Cdr), 2 chevrons with a loop; *Pivsotenniy* (Platoon Cdr), 1 looped chevron; *Bunchuzhnyi* (Company SgtMaj), 3 chevrons; *Chotar* (Ptn Sgt), 2 chevrons; *Roiovyi* (Squad Leader), 1 chevron; *Kozak* (soldier), no device.

Arm-of-service was indicated by devices on the blue collar patches, officially stencilled in yellow and worn above a unit number or name, though few units actually did this; infantry were to wear crossed rifles, cavalry crossed swords and artillery crossed cannons. The *Sich* Rifles had the letters 'CC' (Cyrillic initials for *Sichovi Striltsi*) above rather than below the crossed rifles (see Plate A3).

In **April 1918** a decree abolished the *gimnastiorka* in favour of a tunic styled like the fashionable 'French'; in fact the older garment remained in use. Formal ranks were reintroduced at the same time, but since nobody wanted to return to the old Tsarist shoulder straps the new devices were added to the collar patches. An *Otaman Armii* (General) had an upright mace – an old Ukrainian symbol for a commander – and an 'L'-shaped spray of leaves along the lower edges of the patch, with 2 small stars at the ends of the spray; *Otaman Korpusu* (LtGen), the same with 1 star, on the right; *Otaman Divisii* (MajGen), the same with no star; *Polkovnik* (Col), 2 broad bars below a star; *Osavul* (Deputy Regt Cdr), 2 bars; *Kurinnyi* (LtCol), 1 bar; *Sotnyk* (Capt), 2 narrow bars below a star; *Khorunzhyi* (Lt), 2 narrow braids; and *Pidkhorunzhyi* (2/Lt), 1 narrow braid. All stars were five-pointed. NCOs retained their sleeve chevrons.

Arm-of-service was now indicated by the colour of the collar patch, and by piping around the flaps of the tunic breast pockets and the cuffs, and as trouser or breeches stripes – narrow for men, double with a narrow central piping for officers, and the same but broader for generals. The device (if any) was worn in the lower part of the collar patch below the rank insignia. The colours were: infantry, blue with crossed rifles; cavalry, yellow with crossed swords; artillery, red with a grenade; engineers, black with crossed spade and pickaxe; medical, crimson; and staff, blue. Generals had no devices; General Staff-qualified officers wore the general's leaf spray in addition to their rank and branch device.

The Free Cossacks, clothed by their own villages, wore a variety of outfits, as did many of the volunteer units. Independence had brought with it a wave of enthusiasm for the Cossack style, and a German report dated May 1918 said that many of them wore high fur caps with long 'flames' (i.e. *shlyks* or pointed cloth bags) of a different colour, and that these were intended to make them look purely Ukrainian (see Plate B1). This fashion was also shown in the uniform of the 'Bluecoats', who were given a very distinctive outfit consisting of a long blue fly-fronted *zhupan* with a standing collar, baggy breeches of the same material, and a grey fur cap with a blue *shlyk*. This was worn with a leather waist belt and Cossack-style boots (see Plate B3). This division had its own rank insignia.

The 'Greycoats' wore a shorter version of the *zhupan* with conventional breeches, puttees and a peaked cap, all made of a light grey material; this division also had its own rank insignia (see Plate D1).

THE EX-RUSSIAN UKRAINE:
The Hetmanate, 1918

The Central *Rada* proved unable to maintain order; in chaotic conditions the administration soon lost the confidence of the landowning and business interests. In April 1918 these organized a coup and appointed the conservative Gen Skoropadski (commander of the first Russian corps to have been 'Ukrainianized', and later leader of the Free Cossacks) as *Hetman* of what was now termed the *Ukrainska Derzhava* or Ukrainian State. The Austro-German occupiers, wanting stability above all else, welcomed the coup; Skoropadski co-operated with them, but he was in favour of eventual federation with a White Russia, and the general trend of his regime was towards a greater measure of 'Russification'.

The new state retained the *tryzub* and the national colours, but reversed the flag design to light blue over yellow. The *Sich* Rifles opposed the coup and were

Soldiers of the *Sichovi Striltsi* (*Sich* Rifles) in the service of the Central *Rada*, listening to a *kobzar* – a traditional Ukrainian folk-singer and story-teller. Some still wear their old Austro-Hungarian or Ukrainian Legion uniforms, although most have the new Ukrainian pattern with the 1917 pattern insignia (see left) and St Mikhail cockade.

Members of the Hetmanate's mission to Berlin, 1918. Although the photograph is of poor quality, it is of interest because the standing officer wears the special *zhupan* for the Hetman's ADCs – see Plate C3. The seated official is wearing diplomatic uniform.

disbanded, along with the 'Bluecoats' (their 1st Div was disbanded in Kyiv and the 2nd in Germany or in transit to Ukraine). The main surviving military formation was the *Zaporizhska* Div (three *Zaporozhian* and one *Haidamak* infantry regiments, one artillery and one engineer regiment, a horse-drawn artillery battery, an armoured car regiment and an air squadron). At this point the 'Greycoats' were still forming in Austria-Hungary.

Skoropadski wanted to continue with the *Rada*'s plans for a conscript army, but the Germans prevented this at first. However, another *Serdiuk* (Guard) Div came into existence in July 1918, consisting of the 1st to 4th Infantry Regts, the Lubensky Horse Cossack Regt, an artillery regiment and an engineer company. It was raised from volunteers and 'upper class peasants' in the same way as the Tsarist Guards. The 'Greycoat' Div also arrived in the summer of 1918 – though Skoropadski distrusted it, cut its numbers, and sent it to guard the border with Soviet Russia. It was not until September 1918 that the planned eight corps and four and a half cavalry divisions began to take shape, but by November 1918 the army's strength was 60,000. Most of the officers came from the old Tsarist Army; they provided much-needed expertise, but favoured a 'united and indivisible' Russia rather than Ukrainian independence. Skoropadski also formed a gendarmerie-style State Guard, largely from the old Tsarist police and other White Russians who opposed the idea of independence; this was organized into 139 infantry and 86 cavalry companies.

Hetmanate troops blockaded the Crimea during 1918 when the local Russo-Tartar regime resisted Skoropadski's claim that the peninsula was part of Ukraine. Skoropadski also tried to send the 'Division of General Natiiv' (in fact a detachment of the *Zaporozhian* Div) to the Kuban to liberate this Ukrainian-speaking area, but the Germans prevented the move.

The Hetman's pro-Russian policy provoked internal opposition. The anti-Skoropadski coalition succeeded in forcing him to re-form the *Sich* Rifles in August 1918. By then it was becoming obvious that the Central Powers had lost the war and that Skoropadski could no longer rely on their support. This encouraged his opponents, and after the Armistice in November 1918 they formed a rival body known as the Directory, whose forces were spearheaded by the *Sich* Rifles; the 'Greycoats' also joined the revolt. Although German and Austrian troops were still present in Ukraine, they had no further interest in the war. Most of Skoropadski's own forces went over to the Directory, and he had to turn to the thousands of White Russian officers who had escaped to Ukraine intending to join Denikin's Volunteer Army, which was based in the Don region further to the east. These were assembled into a 'Special Corps' of White Russian officers; Denikin was willing to let them fight for Skoropadski because he distrusted the Ukrainian nationalists, but they were unable to resist the Directory's troops. These took Kyiv in

December 1918, overthrew Skoropadski's regime and forced him into exile. His White Russians rejoined Denikin.

* * *

Uniforms were modified on 21 August 1918. Most arms retained the old *gimnastiorka*, but cavalry and horse artillery enlisted ranks received a new, tunic-style version. Officers wore a tunic with a stand-and-fall collar and four pleated patch pockets: the collar and cuffs could be of a darker khaki. Breeches were khaki (for infantry and engineers) or grey-blue (other arms). The Tsarist greatcoat was retained, and the headdress was a soft peaked cap (see Plate C3). A new metal cockade was introduced in June 1918: round, with a gold fluted edge and a blue central disc bearing a gold *tryzub*. It was made in such quantities that examples were still in use during World War II.

The rank titles and insignia were also altered from **June 1918**. They followed the Tsarist system in having no equivalent of major (a rank discontinued in 1882). The dress shoulder straps resembled the German pattern, being made of gold cords (silver for 2nd and 4th Cavalry Divs, engineers, air troops and support services), with tiny blue chevrons interwoven at intervals, on an underlay of arm-of-service colour. Generals' straps were broad, with four interlaced cords; field officers' straps were narrower, with two central interlaced cords edged with two straight cords; junior officers' straps showed four straight cords. These dress straps bore the same devices as the field pattern.

These field straps differed from the Tsarist pattern in being tapered, with rounded tops, and officers other than generals wore four-sided lozenges rather than stars. The straps themselves were khaki, with braid in a darker shade. Generals had a braid band arranged in zig-zag fashion down the centre of the strap, while those of the other officers had two or one braid strips running down the centre.[4] The ranks were as follows: *Heneralnyi Bunchuzhnyi* (Gen), zig-zag braid with crossed maces; *Heneralnyi Znachkovyi* (LtGen), zig-zag braid with single upright mace; *Heneralnyi Khorunzhyi* (MajGen), zig-zag braid with no device; *Polkovnyk* (Col), double stripe, 2 lozenges; *Vijskovyi Starshina* (LtCol), double stripe, 1 lozenge; *Sotnyk* (Capt), single stripe, 2 lozenges; *Znachkovyi* (Lt), single stripe, 1 lozenge; *Khorunzhyi* (2/Lt), single stripe, no device. Hostilities-only officers of all ranks wore an additional gold or silver braid bar across the base of their straps. Rank was also shown by means of braid breeches stripes, which were broad and double for generals, broad for field officers and narrow for junior officers.

The insignia for conscript NCOs were: *Bunchuznhnyi* (SgtMaj), green edging to strap, green half-loop inside; *Chotovyi* (Sgt), green strap edging; *Roiovyi* (Cpl), green half loop; *Kozak* (soldier), no insignia. Regular NCOs wore yellow insignia and edging: a *Bunchuznhnyi* had a lengthways central stripe and 2 transverse bars; *Chotovyi*, the same, but without bars; *Roiovyi*, edging only.

Regulations issued in June 1918 and expanded in August specified arm-of-service colours, to be worn in the form of piping around the cap crown, collar, shoulder straps, breast pocket flaps and pointed cuffs, as greatcoat collar patches and as officers' breeches stripes. The colours were as follows: Hetman's HQ & Escort, brick-red; General Staff,

Officers of the *Chorni Zaporizhski* ('Black Zaporizhian') Regt in UNR service. Note the *zhupan* coats, black hats, and non-regulation placement of the April 1919 rank insignia. The man on the right wears a death's-head emblem below the national cockade on his cap.

---

4 The illustration of this insignia in the 1930s Ukrainian-language Encyclopaedia is incorrect in a number of respects.

UNR officers, 1920–21. Note the military official (first man standing from the right), with his distinctive collar patches. The second man seated from the left is Col Pavlo Shandruk, future commander of the Ukrainian National Army in 1945.

white, with double crimson breeches stripes; infantry, crimson; cavalry, yellow; artillery and engineers, red; air service, black (with black breeches); justice, green; medical, brown; topographic service, dark blue. Doctors also wore a caduceus on their straps, veterinarians the serpent alone, and pharmacists, twin serpents entwined round a bowl.

Although the basic dress continued to be Russian in style, Skoropadski tried to give representative uniforms a Cossack character (Figure C2). The first of these special uniforms (decreed on 11 August 1918) was for the Lubenski *Serdiuk* Horse Cossack Regiment. The dress version had a low white fur cap with a yellow top and a 'V'-cut in the front, worn with a white plume. The hussar-style jacket was blue, with blue pointed cuffs and five rows of white frogging across the chest, fastening in the centre with toggles. There was a barrel sash, and red breeches with hussar boots. The undress jacket had no frogging and seems to have been hooked closed. The peaked cap was blue with a yellow band and white piping.

This was followed on 3 July by a special uniform for the Hetman's Escort & HQ, extended to the *Serdiuks* on 31 August (although the latter did not actually receive it): a long khaki *zhupan* was worn with a blue-grey peaked cap and breeches, and high boots. The Escort & HQ had a black fur hat with a small white *shlyk*. The *zhupan* was single-breasted with wide skirts which came to mid thigh and were pleated at the back. It had a standing collar, shoulder straps, full sleeves narrowing to tight cuffs, slanting slash pockets with three-point flaps on each side, but no breast pockets; the front fastened with nine small buttons. The collar top, front, pockets, skirts and back seams were edged with dark green braid; this also formed chevrons running upwards from the edges of the cuffs, and nine brandenburgs across the chest. These were plain for the HQ & Escort, but for the *Znachkovi* (the Hetman's ADCs) they ended in small trefoils, with similar trefoils on the fronts of the tunic skirts, in the small of the back, and at the end of the lancer-style braid which arched out across the shoulders at the back (see Plate C1). The rankers' *zhupan* was slightly shorter, and they had no breeches stripes. The *Serdiuk* Div was to have the brandenburgs but without the other braiding. *Serdiuk* units had a special cockade consisting of a 'cross formy' with pointed ends and a disc bearing the *tryzub* in its centre, backed by crossed maces. The Hetman's HQ & Escort wore the standard cockade below crossed maces.

The *Serdiuk* regiments were distinguished by the colours of their cap bands, collar piping, shoulder straps or piping, greatcoat patches, and buttons. The 1st wore crimson with gold buttons; the 2nd, crimson with silver; the 3rd, orange-yellow, the patches piped blue, with gold; and the 4th, the same but with silver buttons.

THE EX-RUSSIAN UKRAINE:
The Directory, 1918–21

In December 1918 the Directory re-established the Ukrainian People's Republic, UNR. It retained the *tryzub* and the Hetman's blue-over-yellow flag. The new regime was soon split by the old struggle between nationalists and Russian federalists; the former won, and the Directory came to be dominated by their leader, the dynamic Simon Petliura. It established friendly relations with Galicia's Western Ukrainian People's Republic (ZUNR – see below), and proclaimed the formation of a joint Ukrainian Republic with the ZUNR as its 'Western Oblast', though further unification measures were postponed.

The UNR was confronted by a formidable array of enemies. To the north-east was a rival 'Red' Ukrainian government supported by the Bolsheviks in Moscow. In the south-east, the White Russian Volunteer Army under Gen Denikin was about to advance northward. Meanwhile, the new Polish government had claimed some UNR territory in Volhynia to the north-west, and its troops were advancing to take possession, while the Rumanians claimed more land to the south-west. Moreover, the victorious Entente, concerned about the new Bolshevik government in Moscow, were anxious to fill the vacuum left by the retreating Austro-German forces, and Entente troops under French command landed at Odesa in December 1918. The Ukrainians opposed them, partly because the French sided with the local White Russians.

The Directory's coup had been spearheaded by the re-formed *Sich* Rifles. The only other formations to survive the Hetmanate's collapse were the *Zaporozhian* Corps and elements of the 'Greycoat' and *Serdiuk* divisions. Other than these, the new regime's forces consisted of a multitude of very small guerrilla units; many of these were short-lived, either disbanding themselves, turning to banditry, or even joining the Reds. They included a Dnipro Insurgent Div (which broke up into separate guerrilla bands at the end of 1918); a *Chornomorska* (Black Sea) Div; a *Selianska* (Peasant) Div from Kyiv province; the *Zaporizhska Sich* (another force raised by an *Otaman* or local warlord); the Volhynian Div (ex-Hetmanate troops); a 1st Galician Regt (Western Ukrainians captured while serving in the Austro-Hungarians); and a Czech 'Ruthenian' regiment. However, some of these 'divisions' only had 400 men; in all, the Directory had roughly 40,000 regular troops and some 100,000 guerrillas.

The Directory decreed universal mobilization, but lacked the means to put this into effect. This encouraged the formation of more semi-independent bands led by local *Otamany* – local leaders who received funds from the Directory and were theoretically subordinate to it, but remained largely autonomous in practice. In an attempt to impose some measure of central control, the main field units were organized into four ad hoc Groups. These were the 'Left Bank

Officers of the UNR's 1st *Ustym Karmal'iuk* Cavalry Bn (centre, its commander Col Igor Trotsky), photographed at Uman in late winter or spring 1919.

Group', which confronted both the Reds and the White Russians to the east; the 'Northern' or 'Right Bank', which fought both the Reds and Polish forces to the north; the 'Southern', which fought the French; and the 'Dnister Group' (effectively the ZUNR army), which fought the Rumanians.

This attempt to fight on four fronts at once was clearly suicidal, and the Directory quickly came to terms with the French and Rumanians, allowing it to transfer its forces north in February 1919. A French liaison mission went to Kyiv, and French and other Entente troops occupied some key towns in the south. The Entente wanted the Ukrainians to co-operate with the Whites, and offered supplies for an army of 300,000; but Denikin refused to negotiate with 'separatists', so fighting with the Whites continued.

Nevertheless, the Reds to the north-east remained the main threat. Fighting broke out on that front early in January 1919, and the Ukrainians were pushed back. Many of the locally raised forces proved unreliable, and the Kyivan Peasant Div actually joined the enemy (though it changed sides again in May). Kyiv fell at the beginning of February 1919, and in March the Reds drove the UNR's main forces back against the Polish forces in Volhynia and cut off their southern units, who were forced to retreat into Rumania and were interned. Meanwhile, separate Red forces operating in the south had pressed the Entente troops back into Odesa. The morale of the Entente expeditionary force was low, and the French command evacuated the port in April, depriving the Directory of a possible ally.

By May 1919 the Directory's forces had been squeezed into a narrow strip of land around Brody. At this point it succeeded in negotiating an armistice with the Poles. Its army was reorganized into three Groups (the *Sich* Rifles, *Zaporizhska* and Volhynian), plus four south-eastern combat groups. With its rear secured by the Polish armistice, it was able to advance south-eastwards to clear the Reds from much of Podilia and to establish the Directory's capital at Kamanets Podil'skyi. Its forces were combined into 12 full-sized divisions, each of three infantry regiments (three battalions each), three of artillery (three batteries each), a technical battalion and a cavalry troop. These divisions were then organized into five Groups: the *Sich* Rifles (the 9th, 10th & 11th Divs, amounting to 4,700 combatants); the *Zaporizhska* (6th, 7th & 8th Divs, with 3,000 men); the Volhynian (1st & 4th Divs with some others, amounting to 4,000); Udovichenko's 3rd 'Iron' Rifles Div of 1,200 combatants; and *Otaman* Tiutiunnik's Group (consisting of the returned Kyiv Peasant Div, *Zaporizhska Sich* and other guerrilla bands reorganized as the 2nd, 5th & 12th Divisions). An attempt to provide each Group with a cavalry brigade and a heavy artillery battery failed for lack of resources.

ABOVE **A group of UNR officers in Poland, 1921. Note the variations in their tunics, and the forage cap worn by one man at the back.**

UNR *Khorunzhyi* (second lieutenant) wearing April 1920 insignia.

As the widely varying strengths indicate, the attempt at standardization was only partially successfully, and the *Sich* Rifles Group remained the best equipped of these formations.

In June 1919 the Directory's troops were joined by the Western Ukrainian People's Republic army (UHA), which had been forced out of Galicia by the advancing Poles. This force retained its own identity.

Meanwhile, in May 1919, Denikin's Whites launched an offensive against the Reds, helped by spontaneous peasant revolts in the latter's rear. His troops pushed them out of much of Eastern and Central Ukraine during the summer and autumn. The Directory forces took advantage of this to advance and reoccupy Kyiv in August, but were immediately expelled again by Denikin's forces. During this campaign the Directory troops and UHA operated as a combined force.

Instead of concentrating on fighting the Reds, Denikin continued to attack the Ukrainians, and succeeded in forcing them back again into a triangle bounded by his own forces to the south, the Poles to the north-west and the Reds to the north-east. The desperate Petliura arranged another armistice with the Poles in September 1919. This led to a split with the Western Ukrainians, who were anti-Polish, and the UHA eventually went over to Denikin's forces in November.

Meanwhile, the Reds had counter-attacked Denikin's forces, whose retreat turned into a rout during October and November, and the resurgent Reds moved back into Ukraine. The Poles also followed Denikin's retreating troops in a south-easterly direction, with the Directory army operating independently beside them, and eventually formed a line which enclosed a portion of the old UNR territory. The Directory forces during this 'Winter March' campaign consisted of 3,000–6,000 men organized into three Groups (*Zaporizhska*, Volhynian and Kyiv), which were renamed divisions in January 1920. Konovalet's *Sich* Rifles (some of them still Galicians) had refused to serve alongside the Poles and had been disbanded. The other units were decimated by a typhus epidemic during November–December 1919, so the survivors retreated north-west and retired behind Polish lines. They were then moved north to the Novograd Volynskyi area to recover.

Denikin's defeat left the Poles and the Reds facing each other, with the Directory as a fairly minor ally of the former. There followed a period of relative calm while both sides gathered their forces. In January 1920 the Poles agreed to help re-form two Ukrainian divisions – the 2nd and 6th, the latter raised from Galician prisoners and internees. A UNR-Polish treaty in April 1920 provided for combined operations under overall Polish command and the re-arming of the UNR army by the Poles. The result was that when the Russo-Polish War flared up again, the re-equipped Directory forces co-operated with the Poles during their Kyiv campaign, the 2nd Div forming part of the Polish 6th Army and the 6th part of the Polish 3rd Army. The joint Polish-Ukrainian force took Kyiv and much of the Right Bank Ukraine, and re-established the Directory in the capital.

The newly restored regime set to work to build up the UNR army yet again. In May 1920 it was reorganized into six divisions: the 1st *Zaporizhska*, 2nd *Volynska*, 3rd *Zalizna* ('Iron'), 4th *Kyivska*, 5th *Khersonska* and 6th *Sichovykh Striltsiv* (so named in honour of the disbanded *Sich* Rifles). Each was to have three brigades with integral artillery, plus one cavalry regiment

OPPOSITE **UNR *Sotnyk* (captain) wearing the sleeve *tryzub* badge as prescribed in July 1919.**

19

UNR *Heneral Poruchchik* (LtGen) Volodymyr Sikevich. Although this photo was taken some 30 years after the Great War, he is still dressed in a so-called *'French'* with 1920 pattern collar patches (for some reason these bear the single star of a major-general). Note the piping of collar, shoulder straps and pocket flaps (cf Plate C1). At his neck he wears the Russian Order of St Vladimir, on his chest the UHA and Simon Petlura crosses.

and a technical regiment, though only the 1st and 6th achieved this structure. A cavalry division was also raised, with six horsed regiments. The units were to be numbered consecutively throughout, though there were inevitably some gaps. An attempt was made to form six reserve brigades to provide reinforcements, but was only partly successful, and they were later formed into a two-brigade machine gun division.

The see-saw Russo-Polish War continued. After a retreat in the face of a Red offensive in summer 1920, the Directory army formed the southernmost wing of the Polish advance that autumn, clearing the Reds out of Galicia again and reoccupying some UNR territory around Kamanets Podil'skyi. Having fought themselves to a standstill, the Poles and the Reds concluded an armistice in November 1920. When this was announced, the disappointed UNR forces launched a unilateral offensive into Soviet-occupied Ukraine, assisted by an isolated White Russian '3rd Army' (one infantry and one cavalry division) which had recognized Ukrainian independence. At this point the UNR army consisted of 39,000 men with 8,000 horses, 675 machine guns, 74 artillery pieces, two armoured trains and three aircraft. This so-called offensive was little more than a large raid and was quickly defeated. The Ukrainians were forced back into Galicia, which duly became Polish territory by the Treaty of Riga of March 1921.

The Ukrainian force remained in being for some time. In October 1921 Petliura's subordinate Tiutiunnik led 1,500 volunteers on another raid into north-west Ukraine, divided into two groups, the Volhynian and the Podilian. This raid too was unsuccessful; and eventually the UNR army's members dispersed. A number of their commanders were taken on as 'contract officers' by the Polish Army.

*   *   *

Uniforms continued to develop under the Directory. Initially there was an attempt to extend Skoropadski's 'national' style to the whole army. A dress uniform decreed on 8 January 1919 consisted of a black fur cap with a white plume, a blue *zhupan* with silver piping down the front, arm-of-service colour cloth belt, collar patches and pointed cuffs, and red breeches. The field uniform decreed at the same time resembled that of the 'Greycoat' Div, with a grey fur cap, *zhupan* and breeches. The *shlyk*, collar patches, cuff piping and breeches stripes were in arm-of-service colours: HQs, brick-red; infantry, crimson; cavalry, yellow; artillery, red; engineers and technical troops, black; medical, brown; and veterinary, violet. A new metal cockade was decreed on 26 January 1919 – a rounded blue oval with a gold *tryzub*, the whole surrounded by a gold band bearing decorative motifs in blue – but this was never actually issued.

The ranks were: *Korpusny Otaman, Divisiyniy Otaman, Brigadniy Otaman* (Corps, Div and Bde Cdrs); *Polkovnik, Vijskovyi Starshina, Kurinnyi* (Regt, Deputy Regt and Bn Cdrs); *Sotnyk, Khorunyi* (Co, Ptn Cdrs); *Bunchuzhnyi, Chotovyi* (Co SgtMaj, Ptn Sgt); *Roiovyi* (Squad Ldr), and *Kozak* (soldier). No official drawings of the insignia seem to have survived, but they appear to have been worn on rectangular collar patches. Those for generals bore zig-zag braid and 3, 2, 1 or no stars; senior officers, 2 forward-slanting braids with 2, 1 or no stars; company officers, 1 braid with 1 or no star; and NCOs, 3, 2, or 1 upright braids.

These uniforms were modified on **24 April 1919**. The dress version was abolished (the authorities recognizing that the situation was too grave for such frivolities). The grey *zhupan* was retained until 30 June as an alternative to the greatcoat, but then disappeared. The new, more orthodox uniform took the form of a khaki peaked cap, tunic and breeches. The tunic had four patch pockets and a vertical band on either side of the chest like a 'Norfolk' shooting jacket (see Plate E2). On 30 June military officials were given a black uniform with an open-collar tunic, white shirt and black tie.

Members of *Otaman* Group 'Orel' (Eagle), c.1919. These guerrillas wear a variety of uniforms, including a *gimnastiorka* on the left. The officers on the extreme right and left are Polish.

Yet another set of rank insignia were introduced, in the form of upward-pointing cuff chevrons, the space between the lowest chevron and the top of the cuff being of arm-of-service colour (see Plate E1). The *Holovnyi Otaman* (C-in-C) wore 2 chevrons, the upper forming a trefoil loop; *Nakazhnnyi Otaman* (Deputy C-in-C), 1 chevron; and War Minister, 3 broad chevrons with a loop above. All three had a trident on the point of the cuff. *Khoshovyi Otaman* (Corps Gen) had 3 broad chevrons with a loop above; *Otaman* (Gen), 2; *Polkovnyk* (Col), 3 medium chevrons; *Osavul* (LtCol), 2; *Sotnyk* (Capt), 3 narrower chevrons with a loop above; *Chotar* (Lt), 2; *Khorunzhyi* (2/Lt), 1; and *Pidkhorunzhyi* (Ensign), 1 without a loop. *Bunchuzhnyi* (SgtMaj) had 4 even narrower chevrons; *Chotovyi* (Sgt), 3; *Roiovyi* (Cpl), 2; *Gurtkovyi* (L/Cpl), 1; and *Kozak* (soldier), no insignia.

Arm-of-service was indicated by the colour of the collar patches and by devices worn on both sides. Some of the colours had been changed: HQ now wore crimson piped with white; infantry, light blue with crossed rifles; cavalry, yellow with crossed swords; artillery, red with crossed cannon; machine-gunners, black with a gun; transport, black with a winged wheel; telegraph, black with a crossed lightning fork; engineers, black with crossed spade and axe; medical, brown with a caduceus; and the air force, cherry-red with either a winged propeller or a balloon. The devices were gilt except for cavalry, who wore silver. General Staff officers wore black patches with white piping. After 30 September graduates of the Imperial Russian General Staff Academy wore black with piping in the colour of the arm or service in which they were currently serving.

UNR junior officers in varieties of winter field dress, 1920.

The insignia were modified yet again on **30 July 1919**. The June 1918 cockade was reintroduced – the gilt *tryzub* on a blue disc surrounded by gilt fluting. The arm-of-service collar patches were discontinued, and both rank and arm-of-service devices were now to be worn directly on the collar, the former on the right hand side and the latter on the left. Generals wore their insignia on both sides. The ranks were as follows: *Holovnyi Otaman* (C-in-C), a trident within a half-wreath; *Otaman* (Gen), trident set on a vertical stripe halved blue

UNR *Kozak* (private) from the *Sich* Rifles in March 1919, wearing the Russian version of the Adrian helmet, with a death's-head badge painted on the front.

Otaman Bojko, the independently minded commander of the *Zaporizhska Sich* who helped himself to some Cossack relics from a museum, is at front centre in fleece cap and long *zhupan*. The collar patches worn by the officer left of him, on a greatcoat, are the only known illustrations of the January 1919 rank insignia.

and yellow; *Polkovnyk* (Col), 2 vertical bars with 2 studs behind; *Osavul* (LtCol), 2 bars, 1 stud; *Sotnyk* (Capt), 1 bar, 3 studs in triangle; *Chotar* (Lt), 1 bar, 2 studs; *Khorunzhyi* (SubLt), 1 bar, 1 stud; and *Pidkhorunzhyi* (Ens), 1 bar. The *Bunchuzhnyi* (SgtMaj) wore 4 studs in a rectangle; *Chotovyi* (Sgt), 3 studs; *Roiovyi* (Cpl), 2 studs; *Gurtkovyi* (L/Cpl), 1 stud.

Arm-of-service was now to be shown by a cloth *tryzub* in the appropriate colour on the left sleeve. The collar devices appear to have remained unchanged, as did most arm-of-service colours. Railway troops had worn green from 24 April, and General Staff an oakleaf on their white-piped black trident.

Extraordinary as it seems, the ranks and devices were modified once more on **16 April 1920**. Arm-of-service colour collar patches were reintroduced, now with triple-pointed rear ends. A *Heneral Polkovnyk* (ColGen) had a wreathed trident with 3 stars to the rear; *Heneral Poruchnyk* (LtGen), the same with 2 stars; *Heneral Khorunzhyi* (MajGen), the same with 1 star; *Polkovnyk* (Col), 3 horizontal bars; *Pidpolkovnyk* (LtCol), 2 bars; *Sotnyk* (Capt), 3 stars over 1 bar; *Poruchnyk* (1/Lt), 2 stars, 1 bar; *Khorunzhyi* (2/Lt), 1 star, 1 bar; *Piokhorunyi* (Ensign/Warrant Officer), 1 bar; *Bunchuzhnyi* (SgtMaj), 5 stars; *Chotovyi* (Sgt), 4 stars; *Roiovyi* (Cpl), 3 stars; *Gurtkovyi* (L/Cpl), 2 stars; *Kozak* (soldier), 1 star. These devices were gold for combat arms, and silver for HQ staff and services. Military officials and other non-combatants wore rectangular patches with silver devices.

There was undoubtedly a good deal of variety in practice. Stars with five, six and occasionally even seven points were worn, and photographs show that officers' tunics varied in the number of buttons and styles of pocket flap. The soldiers wore an even wider variety of outfits. Pavlo Shandruk notes that in early 1919 only one in ten men of his unit had good shoes, and that most wore civilian clothing, though he later succeeded in obtaining uniforms and steel helmets for them in Kyiv. Later in the same year he had to give another unit heavy white shirts, with shoes made from tarpaulin material. The steel helmets were of the Russian 'Adrian' pattern, with the *tryzub* (or occasionally a death's-head) painted on the front in black or yellow.

THE WESTERN UKRAINIAN PEOPLE'S REPUBLIC (ZUNR), 1918–20

Following the defeat of the Austro-Hungarian Empire, its subject peoples all tried to assert their independence. A Ukrainian *Rada* in Galicia did so in November 1918, and formed the *Zakhidno Ukrainska Narodnia Republika* or ZUNR (Western Ukrainian People's Republic). The flag was horizontal stripes of light blue over yellow – the reverse of the original UNR

arrangement. The *tryzub* was adopted as the state symbol, though the Galician lion sometimes replaced it.

The Polish section of the population immediately rebelled and called for help from the new Polish government in Warsaw. Galicia had been Polish territory before it became part of Austria, so the Poles claimed the province again and sent troops to help the rebels.

The ZUNR's army was known as the *Ukrainska Halytska Armiia* or UHA (Ukrainian Galician Army). Its nucleus was provided by the legionaries of the Ukrainian *Sich* Rifles, who were reinforced by Ukrainians from other Austro-Hungarian units and by a number of local guerrilla detachments. The basic unit was the battalion-sized *kuren*, three to five of which formed a Group, though there was little uniformity of either organization or equipment. Universal conscription was decreed in November 1918, and a territorial organization of three military districts (Lviv, Ternopil and Stanyslaviv). The new army was organized along Austro-Hungarian lines, though there was a shortage of staff officers and the ex-Russian UNR army had to provide two of the UHA's commanders. In December 1918 the Groups were placed under a central command, and in January 1919 they began to be combined into three Corps. Each had four brigades (of two to five battalions, and an artillery regiment of three to five batteries with four to six guns each), a cavalry detachment, an engineer unit and service units. The battalion had four rifle companies and a MG company. There were 45 battalions and 40 artillery batteries, but the weak cavalry was limited to several detachments of 40–50 men each. The artillery arm was relatively powerful, being equipped with Austrian 75mm, 78mm and 105mm field guns and 100mm or 122mm howitzers; each regiment also had a heavy battery of two 155mm guns.

The 1st Corps had the 5th Sokal, 6th Rava Ruska, 9th Uhniv (later Belz) and 10th Yaniv or Yavoriv Brigades; the 2nd Corps, the 1st Ukrainian *Sich* Rifles, 2nd Kolomyia, 3rd Berezhany and 4th Zolochiv Bdes; the 3rd Corps, 7th Stryi (later Lviv), 8th Sambir, 11th Stryi, 12th and 1st Mountain Brigades. In April 1919 the 2nd Corps brigades were reorganized into two regiments of three *kurens* each, and in June new 4th and 5th Corps were organized, though these were quickly disbanded for lack of manpower.

The main battles fought by the UHA were for possession of Lviv and the other towns. The more urbanized Poles managed to hold on to these, and in April 1919 the arrival of Haller's French-equipped 'Blue Army' gave them a decisive advantage. Although the Poles remained the main enemy, the ZUNR also claimed Bukovyna, and this brought them into conflict with the Rumanians. The latter attacked in the south in May, forcing the UHA to retreat. It counter-attacked the Poles in June, but they recovered in July and forced the main UHA body out of Galicia and into UNR territory. The UHA's Mountain Bde had already been cut off by the Haller offensive and forced to retreat into Czechoslovakia. It helped the Czechs to fight Bela Kun's Hungarians and was then reorganized as the 'Ukrainian Bde'; the Czechs maintained it for a period, fearing conflict with the Poles, but dissolved it in the early 1920s.

Meanwhile, the main body of the UHA crossed into the ex-Russian Ukraine and joined the UNR forces. However, the latter's action in allying themselves with the Poles led to the Galicians going over to Denikin's forces in November 1919 (the White Russians had no claim on

Heneral Chetar (MajGen) Wolf of the Western Ukrainian Army (UHA), 1919. This clearly shows the *tryzub* cap cockade, and the maces of the general officers' rank insignia, although his sleeve braid is not quite regulation. Note the distinctive shape of the pocket flaps – cf Plate A.

Galicia). Denikin's Whites were in full retreat by this period, and the UHA found itself short of supplies and, like the UNR army, weakened by the typhus epidemic of November 1919.

In January 1920 it went over to the Reds and became the 'Red UHA'. In March this was reorganized to form three brigades (each with three regiments of three battalions, one artillery regiment, one heavy artillery battery and one cavalry regiment). The old 2nd Corps became the 1st Red Ukrainian *Sich* Rifles Bde, the 1st Corps the 2nd Bde and the 3rd Corps the 3rd Brigade. These formed part of the Red army which confronted the joint Polish-Ukrainian forces at the start of the latter's Ukraine campaign in April 1920. The 2nd and 3rd Bdes promptly changed sides again, and the 1st Bde surrendered after being surrounded. Most of the men were interned, but some joined the UNR army's 6th Division. When the Poles retreated again in June, they crossed into Czechoslovakia and were interned there.

* * *

The early UHA forces wore a mixture of Austro-Hungarian **uniforms** and civilian dress. A new grey-green uniform prescribed in April 1919 resembled that of the Ukrainian *Sich* Rifles of 1917. Originally it included the *Mazepynka kappi* with arm-of-service piping, but only the 1st Bde actually wore this, the others adopting a round peaked cap with an arm-of-service-colour band. The tunic had visible buttons and four patch pockets, and was worn with breeches and either field boots or puttees (see Plate F2). The equipment was Austro-Hungarian. The 1st Bde's cavalry squadron wore fur caps and slung pelisses (see Plate F1).

The cockade was blue with a gold rim and *tryzub*; officers seem to have worn an embroidered version with the outer part of coiled gold cord, and some versions had a Galician lion in the centre instead of the trident.

Rank insignia took the form of horizontal cuff stripes, extending from the back seam only part way towards the front, on arm-of-service colour backing. A *Heneral Sotnyk* (Gen) had a broad band of lozenge-pattern silver lace ending in a gold rosette, flanked by gold crossed maces, plus 2 narrower and slightly shorter flanking stripes. *Heneral Poruchnyk* (LtGen) had one such stripe below the broad band, and *Heneral Chetar* (MajGen) the broad band only. *Polkovnyk* (Col) had 3 medium plaited gold bands ending in rosettes; *Pidpolkovnyk* (LtCol) and *Otaman* (Maj), 2 and 1 bands. *Sotnyk* (Capt) had 3 flat gold lace bands ending in rosettes; *Poruchnik* (1/Lt) and *Chotar* (2/Lt), 2 and 1 such bands, and *Khorunzhyi* (Ens), 1 very narrow grey-green band. A *Bulavnyi Starshyi Desiatnyk* (SgtMaj) had 1 broad and 1 narrow band of silver lace, pointed at the forward end, without rosettes; *Starshyi Desiatnyk* (S/Sgt), 1 broad band; *Desiatnyk* (Sgt), 3 narrow; *Vistun* (Cpl), 2; *Starshyi Strilets* (Pte 1st Class), 1; and *Strilets* (Pte), no insignia. Officers wore gold lace chin straps on the cap, and other ranks green leather; officers had gold sword knots, and NCOs yellow.

The *zubchatka* or collar patch had a distinctive zig-zag edge ('wolf's teeth') and varied according to rank and branch. Generals had a silver *zubchatka* on a rectangular gold base; field officers, arm-of-service colour on the same colour base; junior officers, arm-of-service colour edged with gold lace; and NCOs and men, a plain zig-zag (see Plate F). Arm-of-service was also shown by the colour of the cap band and cuff stripe edging. General Staff wore crimson; infantry, blue; cavalry, yellow; artillery, red; engineers, dark yellow; technical, ash-grey; transport, dark green; medical,

(continued on page 33)

WORLD WAR I
1: Volunteer, Legion of Ukrainian *Sich* Rifles, 1914
2: NCO, Legion of Ukrainian *Sich* Rifles, 1917
3: Junior officer, Galician-Bukovynian Battalion of *Sich* Rifles;
   Kyiv, spring 1918

1   3   2

A

THE UNR
1: Volunteer, Battalion of Red Haidamaks,
   Haidamak Host of NE Ukraine; winter 1918
2: Soldier, Ivan Bogun Regiment, winter 1918
3: Private, 1st Ukrainian 'Bluecoat' Division, March 1918

1

2

3

B

THE HETMANATE
1: Captain, 1st *Serdiuk* (Guards) Inf Regt, 1918
2: *Hetman* Pavlo Skoropadski, 1918
3: Personal ADC to the Hetman, 1918

THE DIRECTORY
1: Major, HQ 1st Cossack Rifle 'Greycoat' Div, 1918–19
2: Commander, Guerrilla Detachment Bojko, 1919
3: Private, Black *Zaporozhian* Cav Regt, 1919

1   2   3

D

1: General Staff officer, 1919
2: Simon Petlura, Commander-in-Chief, 1919
3: Officer, 1st *Gutusul* Marine Regt, 1919

E

THE ZUNR
1: Cavalryman, 1st Brigade, UHA, 1919
2: Lieutenant-colonel, UHA cavalry, 1919
3: Sergeant-major, People's Guard, 1919

1

2

3

F

WORLD WAR II
1: Junior officer, Carpathian *Sich*, 1939
2: Officer, 'Roland' Battalion, 1941
3: NCO of a Ukrainian Security Battalion, c.1942

G

WORLD WAR II & AFTER
1: Private, Ukrainian Liberation Army, 1943–44
2: Major, Ukrainian National Army, 1945
3: Commander, Ukrainian Insurgent Army, 1949

1

2

3

black; veterinary, brown; transport, dark green; communications, blue-green; supply, maroon; military officials, light bronze; gendarmerie, brick-red; and aviation first grey, then white.

Specialist badges in the form of initials such as 'SS' (*skorostrilnik* or machine-gunner) were worn above the left elbow. Later, formation insignia appeared on the right forearm, brigades wearing a cross with the upright in the corps' colour and the underlying horizontal bar in the brigade's. These colours were: 1st, red; 2nd, blue; 3rd, yellow; 4th, green; and 5th, white. Corps artillery replaced the horizontal bar with a red disc, and cavalry with a yellow triangle.

The UHA retained its original uniforms while fighting alongside the UNR forces. When it became the Red UHA the cockade was changed to the Red Army's red star and the Galician rank insignia were abolished.

UHA privates with, at right, a *Khorunzhyi* (ensign); note the latter's cuff stripe and, just visible, the narrow braid edging to his *zubchatka* collar patches.

Bukovyna and Carpathia, 1918–19

The Ukrainians in Bukovyna wanted to join the ZUNR, but the province was occupied by Rumanian troops in November 1918 and the UHA was too committed to the Polish campaign to oppose them. A battalion of Bukovynian volunteers fought with it in 1918–19.

The Ukrainians (Ruthenians) in ex-Hungarian Carpathia were divided: some wanted to join the ZUNR, some Hungary, but Czech occupation ensured that the pro-Czechoslovak faction won the day in May 1919. No local uniforms or insignia are known.

UKRAINIAN GUERRILLA FORCES, 1918–24

Ukrainian guerrilla bands were active during the Civil War period. Some claimed to be loyal to the Ukrainian state, but others acknowledged no allegiance, and all fought both the Red and White Russians with equal ferocity. After 1920 they constituted the only Ukrainian forces left in the Soviet Ukraine. At that date they were said to number some 40,000; some of them fought on until 1924.

The largest and best known of these groups was that of the peasant Anarchist leader Nestor Makhno, who began operations in the south-eastern Ukraine against the Hetmanate regime in July 1918. In September he formed a 'Ukrainian Insurrectionary Army' with arms and equipment obtained from the retreating Austro-German troops. He fought Denikin's Whites until they retreated in late 1919, then continued to fight the Reds until his forces were defeated and dispersed in August 1921. Makhno himself managed to slip across the Rumanian border.

In mid 1919 the 'Ukrainian Insurrectionary Army' had a strength of some 15,000 men organized into one cavalry and four infantry brigades, a machine gun regiment with 500 guns, and an artillery detachment. At its peak in late 1919 it had at least 25,000 men with 48 field guns, four armoured trains, four armoured cars and 1,000 machine guns. It was organized into divisions of three brigades, each of three regiments with three battalions. One of these divisions is reported to have had the title 'Iron', but no detailed order of battle is known.

In the nature of things, these guerrilla bands wore little by way of **uniform**. Makhno's troops operated under the black Anarchist flag; their dress was variegated and does not appear to have been subject to any form of regulation.

THE UKRAINIAN SOCIALIST SOVIET REPUBLIC, 1917–21

When the *Rada* proclaimed Ukrainian independence in December 1917, the Bolsheviks formed a rival 'Ukrainian People's Republic' in Karkhiv, which Moscow recognized as an independent state. The Bolshevik forces operating in Ukraine were subordinated to this new government in February 1918 as the 'Army of the Ukrainian Republic', amounting to five weak 'armies' of some 2,000 men each. Although they undoubtedly contained a substantial number of Ukrainians, they remained under the effective control of Moscow.

The Red forces were driven out by the Central Powers, and it was not until November 1918 that Moscow formed a 'Ukrainian Front' of two Russian and two Ukrainian divisions to reconquer Ukraine. The latter were the 1st and 2nd Ukrainian Soviet Divs, the 1st based on the *Tarashcha* and *Bohun* regiments. In January 1919 they were reinforced by further Russian formations and soon succeeded in regaining most of the territory. Various *Otaman* groups joined the Red forces and succeeded in retaining their separate identities for a time, though all were eventually absorbed.

The restored Red government took the name Ukrainian Socialist Soviet Republic (UkSSR) in January 1919, and began to form a Ukrainian Workers' and Peasants' Red Army (UkRSChA), which by mid-1919 had some 100,000 men. In June, however, responsibility for defence was transferred to Moscow, and the UkRSChA was disbanded, the men going to form the Red Army's 12th and 14th Armies. This policy displeased many Ukrainian Communists.

During autumn 1919 Denikin's White Russians overran most of Ukraine, but the Red Army's 8th and 13th Armies reoccupied it during December. These contained no specifically Ukrainian formations other than some Bolshevik guerrillas and Anarchist allies. The Galician UHA joined the Reds in January 1920, and retained its separate identity for a while.

The only other Ukrainian troops in the Red Army during this period were the 'Red Cossacks of Ukraine', who began as a regiment and then became a brigade in 1919. During the Russo-Polish War the UkSSR authorities arranged for it to be transferred from the Baltic area to the Ukrainian front, where it was expanded into a division (later a corps), and 'Ukrainianized'.

The Anarchist guerrilla leader Nestor Makhno (seated) with some of his followers. Embroidered sashes, and revolvers – all carefully pointed towards the right of the photograph – are very much in evidence.

The 1918 state flag was red with blue and yellow stripes in the canton; that of 1919 was red with the letters 'YCCP' in yellow. No specifically Ukrainian **uniforms** or insignia are known. Paustovski (who was conscripted into the UkRSChA in 1919) met an officer who wore a red tunic, purple riding breeches with a silver stripe, red boots, red gloves, and a Cossack hat with a scarlet top – though the army's normal dress was undoubtedly much drabber.

THE INTER-WAR YEARS

The Ukrainian Socialist Soviet Republic from 1921

The Ukraine-based forces remained part of the Red Army after 1921, but their commander was an ex-officio member of the UkSSR's government. In 1924 'Ukrainianization' became official policy; the republic's four territorial cavalry and ten infantry divisions all drew their recruits from Ukraine, and used Ukrainian as the language of command.

This policy was reversed at the end of the 1920s. The territorial system was abolished in 1934, and the 'national' units were broken up; thereafter Ukrainian recruits were sent to mixed Red Army formations. There were no specifically Ukrainian units during World War II other than local defence units, and the '1st Ukrainian Guerrilla Div' formed in autumn 1943 and used mostly against the Ukrainian nationalist partisans.

Normal Soviet **uniforms** were worn, with no specifically Ukrainian insignia.

Ukrainians in other East European Armies, 1921–39

Ukrainian-speakers in Czechoslovakia, Poland and Rumania were subject to conscription. There were no specifically Ukrainian units in any of these armies, though the Czechoslovak 12th Div in Transcarpathia contained a high proportion of 'Ruthenians'. However, the Poles took on a number of Ukrainian exiles as 'contract officers', and encouraged them to prepare plans for the raising of an allied Ukrainian army in the event of another Russo-Polish war. This was to have four infantry and one cavalry divisions, and it was hoped that the Red Army's own Ukrainian formations could be won over to the cause.

These plans were continually revised during the 1930s. The designated Ukrainian commander, Pavlo Shandruk (at once both a Polish lieutenant-colonel and a Ukrainian major-general), writes that in September 1939 he was charged with raising two brigades of Ukrainians to help defend Galicia against the expected Soviet invasion, but that Poland was overrun before these could be formed.

Czech, Polish and Rumanian **uniforms** were worn, and there were no specifically Ukrainian insignia.

Carpatho-Ukraine, 1938–39

The province of Subcarpathian Ruthenia formed the easternmost tip of Czechoslovakia. After the Munich Agreement of September 1938 it was given internal

Two members of the Carpathian *Sich*. In this case there is piping round the *Mazepynka kappis* and the cuffs. Other photographs show collar patches or devices; clearly, *Sich* uniforms were still developing when the Hungarian invasion put an end to the process.

1938	**Carpatho-Ukraine**		**E.(Russian) Ukraine**
Sept	Subcarpathian Ruthenia becomes autonomous following		Germans form Ukrainian Liberation Army (UVV)
	Munich Agreement	July	Soviets begin drive to recapture Ukraine
1939	Carpatho-Ukraine proclaimed an independent state;	Nov	Soviets recapture Kyiv
	repulses Czech attack, but then attacked and annexed	**1944**	
	by Hungary	July	**W.Ukraine (Galicia)**
	W.Ukraine (Galicia)		Soviets take Lviv
Sept	Germany invades Poland. Nazi-Soviet Pact gives Galicia	Nov	**Carpatho-Ukraine**
	to the USSR		Soviets take Carpatho-Ukraine
1941		**1945**	
June	Germany invades USSR and occupies Galicia, which	Mar	Germans recognize Ukrainian 'independence' in respect
	becomes part of Polish *Generalgouvernement*		of all three territories, and Ukrainian National Army (UNA)
	E.(Russian) Ukraine		is formed.
	German-occupied Soviet Ukraine becomes	Apr	Germany surrenders
	Reichskommissariat Ukraine.	June–	Galicia & Carpatho-Ukraine are formally incorporated into
	In both territories the UPA (Insurgent Army) is formed.	Aug	Ukrainian Soviet Socialist Republic, finally uniting all
1943			Ukrainian lands – but under Soviet Russian control. The
Apr	**W.Ukraine (Galicia)**		UPA remains in existence and continues to resist until
	Germans begin to raise local *Polizei* and *Waffen-SS* units		mid-1950s.

self-government as Carpatho-Ukraine. It adopted the light blue-over-yellow flag, and a coat of arms consisting of a shield divided vertically, with a red bear on a silver field on the left, blue and yellow stripes on the right, and the *tryzub*. In October 1938 the regional government created a voluntary militia called the *Karpatska Sich* (Carpathian *Sich*). This had five permanent garrisons which conducted training. There was a *Sich* command, several *kosh* (regional commands), and a number of *viddil* (detachments), which could be combined to form *kurin* (battalions). By February 1939 the *Sich* had about 15,000 members, though its effective strength was only about 2,000.

In March 1939 the government declared independence. Czech forces tried to suppress this, but the Carpathians forced them to withdraw. However, the Hungarians then claimed the province, which had been part of Hungary up to 1918, and launched an invasion. The *Sich* put up a brief resistance before being overrun, and the little state was then incorporated into Hungary.

The *Sich* adopted military-style **uniforms** in February 1939. Some of the leadership wore this in blue-grey, but the regulation colour was grey-green, with a 'V'-fronted *Mazepynka kappi*, a four-button tunic with open collar, and breeches (see Plate G1). In practice many members only had *Mazepynka kappis* and blue/yellow brassards to go with their civilian clothing. Although some individuals may have worn small cockades, collar patches, or a yellow *tryzub* on a blue sleeve shield, details of the insignia remain obscure, and the limited photographic evidence suggests that there was little standardization. The ranks were *Otaman* (Commander), *Sotnyk* (Company Cdr), *Chotar* (Platoon Cdr); *Desiatnyk* ('commander of ten', NCO); *Starshiy Sichovyk* (Sen Pte) and *Sichovyk* (Private). The *Sich's* arms and equipment were of Czech patterns.

WORLD WAR II

Ukrainian units in the German forces, 1939–45

Before the war Ukrainians believed the Germans to be sympathetic to their nationalist hopes, since Germany had been one of the first countries to recognize Ukrainian independence in 1918, and was also the most likely opponent of both Poland and Soviet Russia. The exiled Organization of Ukrainian Nationalists (OUN) was based in Germany during the 1930s, and had contacts with the German Foreign Ministry.

In September 1939 the German *Abwehr* (military intelligence branch) allowed the OUN to form a battalion-sized Legion composed of 600 ex-members of the Carpathian *Sich*. This 'Sushko Legion' (named after its commander) accompanied the German forces during their invasion of Poland, but was then disbanded following the Russo-German Pact.

By the start of Operation 'Barbarossa' in June 1941 the *Abwehr* had formed a volunteer Ukrainian battalion known as *'Nachtigall'* as part of its Brandenburg Regiment. Another battalion, known as *'Roland'*, had been formed in Austria. The two units were known to the Ukrainians as *Druzhyny Ukraninskykh Natsionalistiv* (Ukrainian Nationalist Units, DUN). *Nachtigall* accompanied German forces into Galicia, and *Roland* moved into the southern Soviet Ukraine. However, they were withdrawn to Germany after the OUN's premature proclamation of Ukrainian independence on 30 June 1941 in Lviv. A compromise was reached whereby they agreed to serve as allies (i.e. without taking an oath of allegiance to Hitler), whereupon they were sent to perform anti-partisan duties in Byelorussia in October 1941. When their one-year term of service expired they refused to re-engage and were disbanded, the officers being arrested and many of the men joining the Ukrainian Insurgent Army, UPA (see below). *Nachtigall's* commander, Capt Shukhevych, escaped and became the UPA's commander under the *nom de guerre* of Taras Chuprynka.

When the Germans overran Ukraine in 1941 they were greeted as liberators, and although their racially inspired policies quickly dismayed the nationalists the German cause nevertheless continued to attract considerable support. The Germans added Galicia to their *Generalgouvernement* (occupied Poland), and formed a special Ukrainian police force, based on the regular Polish police but with a new national emphasis. The ex-Soviet Ukraine became the *Reichskommisariat Ukraine*, except for those areas immediately to the rear of the front line.

The local security structure in the Ukrainian territories seems to have been complicated to begin with, and was made even more so by changes over the passage of time, whereby a number of initially autonomous groups came under closer German control and then – as both

A rare photograph showing members of the Sushko Legion sponsored by the *Abwehr*, which served with the German forces in Poland in 1939. After it was disbanded following the Nazi-Soviet pact many of them joined the German-controlled police or other para-military organizations. The value of this blurred image lies in its confirmation of the use of modified Czech tunics and field caps.

Ukraine, 1939–55

Members of a Ukrainian *Schuma* unit in German service. They wear the early black uniform with either pale green or pale blue collars, cuffs, and in some cases skirt pocket flaps; but most have field-grey or khaki forage caps. Note the variety of rifles carried, including a semi-automatic Tokarev SVT-38.

were forced out of Ukraine by the Soviet advance – incorporated into the *Wehrmacht* or *Waffen-SS*. The *Ukrainska Dopomizhna Politsiia* (UDP), Ukrainian Auxiliary Police, were the ex-Soviet Ukrainian police, who carried out normal constabulary duties. They were supported by the *Ukrainska Okhoronna Politsiia* (UOP), Ukrainian Protection Police, and the *Ukrainska Poriaadkova Politsiia* (UPP), Ukrainian Order Police. A number of semi-autonomous local self-defence and auxiliary police forces appeared in both Galicia and the *Reichskommisariat* following the German takeover. These were generally known as the *Ukrainska Narodna Samooborona* (UNS). There were also *Samooboronni Kushchevi Viddily* (SKV), Self-Defence Bush Detachments, and special guard units called *Okhoronni Promyslovi Viddily* (OPV), which were set up to protect factories. In many cases these bodies doubled as units of the OUN's resistance network.

Some of these units were subsequently incorporated into the *Schutzmannschaften der Ordnungspolizei* or 'Schuma', the auxiliary paramilitary police force created in November 1941 to serve under German Higher SS & Police Leaders in the occupied territories. One example of this process was the *Ukrainskyi Legion Samooboronni* (ULS), Ukrainian Legion of Self-Defence, which was formed in 1943 from auxiliary police units in Volhynia and Kholm and which became the 31st *Schuma* Bn in mid-1944. There were about 71 Ukrainian *Schuma* battalions in all, raised at different times for anti-partisan purposes, and including some Cossack and artillery units. The *Schuma* was divided into *Front* and *Wacht* units, the former intended for active anti-partisan operations and the latter for static guard duties.

In April 1943 the Germans decided to raise a number of *Polizei-Schutzen* regiments; their 1st Battalions were to be German, the 2nd and 3rd of *Ostvolk*, preferably Ukrainians. Regiments Nos.31 to 38 were formed, though Nos.31 & 32 were quickly disbanded again.

At the same time the *Waffen-SS* was persuaded to raise a combat division from Galician Ukrainians, whose loyalty to the Habsburg Emperor had not been forgotten. Himmler stipulated that recruits had to be of the Greek Catholic faith to ensure that they were in fact Galicians (most of the Russian Ukrainians were Orthodox). This formation became the *14. SS-Freiwilligen Division 'Galizien'* – to the Ukrainians, *Dyviziia Halychyna*. From autumn 1943 its infantry regiments became the 29th, 30th & 31st as part of a general *Waffen-SS* renumbering. Far more volunteers came forward than were needed, so the surplus were formed into five *Galizisches SS-Freiwilligen Regiment (Polizei)*, Nos.4 to 8. These were disbanded and the men drafted into the division during 1944, though not before they had seen some combat in France. Elements of the 14. SS-Division went into action at Brody in mid-1944 and were almost annihilated. The division was subsequently rebuilt; however, many of the new recruits were Soviet Ukrainians, and in November 1944 this fact was recognized by a change of title to *14. Waffen Grenadier Division der SS (ukrainische Nr.1)*.[5]

5 See MAA 415, *The Waffen-SS (3): 11. to 23. Divisions.*

The German Army also recruited a considerable number of Ukrainians from among their Polish and Soviet prisoners of war and from local volunteers. Unlike the corresponding Russian Army of Liberation, there were few specifically Ukrainian units, and although there are said to have been some 180,000 Ukrainians serving with the *Wehrmacht* in all, most of them remained scattered between various German units. In 1943 these men became part of a new *Ukrainske Vyzvolne Vijsko* (UVV), Ukrainian Liberation Army, but their incorporation into a national army was largely nominal. Some of the UVV battalions posted to France even joined the *maquis* as its *Ivan Bohun* and *Taras Shevchenko* battalions, being transferred to the Foreign Legion's 13e DBLE and RMLE in 1944 (they had reportedly worn Ukrainian national colours superimposed on their French tricolour brassards).

ABOVE **Officers of the *Roland* Battalion, 1941, with its commander in the foreground. They wear Czech uniform but with *zubchatkas* on the collars and their own rank insignia on the cuffs.**

Apart from some use of 'booty' or captured items, the arms and equipment were German throughout.

* * *

The 1939 Ukrainian Legion wore Czech **uniforms** re-dyed green. No contemporary insignia can be confirmed, though veterans later wore a commemorative breast badge bearing the OUN device (the *tryzub* with an upright sword as its central shaft). In 1941 *'Nachtigall'* wore *Wehrmacht* uniforms, to which some members added blue and yellow shoulder loops. A blurred but interesting group photo seems to show M1940 enlisted men's uniform, retaining German shoulder straps, collar bars, and in some cases the breast eagle; the field caps do not seem to bear insignia. *'Roland'* wore ex-Czech uniforms with UHA-style insignia, including the characteristic *zubchatka* on the collar (see Plate G2).

BELOW **Ukrainian *Waffen-SS Sturmmann*/NCO candidate wearing the yellow-on-blue armshield of the 14th Galician Division.**

The *Generalgouvernement*'s Ukrainian Police wore a blue uniform consisting of a *Mazepynka kappi*, a closed-collar tunic with four pockets, breeches and black field boots. The *kappi* had a cloth peak, a silver (officers) or black (other ranks) strap, and red piping around the band, which was cut away at the front in the traditional 'V'-shape. The circular blue cockade bore a gold *tryzub*. On the right sleeve all ranks wore a cuff band bearing the title 'GENERALGOUVERNEMENT' in silver (officers) or white (other ranks) on red, edged with green, and also with silver for officers. All ranks also wore a red *zubchatka* collar patch which was edged with silver for officers. Ranks were shown on the shoulder strap. Officers had red straps edged with silver: a *Major* displayed a zig-zag of silver braid; *Hauptmann*, 2 silver 8-point stars; *Oberleutnant*, 1 star; and *Leutnant* a plain strap. NCOs wore blue straps edged with red: an *Obermeister* had broad silver *Tresse* braid all round and 1 silver 8-point star; *Meister*, braid only; *Hauptwachtmeister*, a blue strap with 1 broad and 1 narrow silver bar; and *Wachtmeister*, 1 broad bar only.[6]

There are no known details of the various local police uniforms except that the UDP are reported to have worn

6 See MAA 412, *Partisan Warfare 1941–5*, Plate A1.

An *Oberleutnant* of the *Generalgouvernement* Police in occupied Poland. The breast badge shows him to be a former member of the Sushko Legion; in bronze, this bore a *tryzub* with a sword as its shaft.

yellow-over-blue brassards. The early auxiliary units generally wore either Red Army or civilian clothing with the insignia removed, and a brassard reading '*Im Dienste der Deutsches Wehrmacht*' in black on white or field-grey.

To begin with, *Schuma* recruits wore a mixture of items. In 1942 they were issued with black sidecaps and *Allgemeine-SS* uniforms modified by the addition of German 'Police green' lapels, shoulder straps, pocket flaps and deep cuffs. In practice it appears that many of these facings were actually light blue, though it is not clear whether there was any connection with the Ukrainian colours. Although no cap badge was prescribed, many Ukrainian members adopted a blue circular cockade with a gold *tryzub* and edge. From May 1942 NCOs used a combination of silver bars and chevrons on the lower left sleeve as rank insignia, while officers wore silver collar insignia.

Later in 1942, field-grey uniforms began to be issued to the *Front* battalions. The cap badge was a wreathed swastika, while a similar but larger badge incorporating the legend 'TREU-TAPFER-GEHORSAM' was worn on the left sleeve. The badges were originally of the branch colour (light green for urban police, orange for gendarmerie and crimson for firemen), but the colours were later standardized as green-grey or white on black. NCOs now wore their ranks in the form of braid collar chevrons. Many men continued to wear the *tryzub* cockade.

The Ukrainian *Polizei-Schutzen* regiments wore the normal German 'Police green' (later field-grey) field uniform without specifically Ukrainian insignia, as did the *SS-Polizei* regiments. The 14. SS-Division wore standard *Waffen-SS* uniform with an armshield of a yellow rampant lion between three crowns on a blue ground; this was supposed to be worn on the upper right arm but in practice appeared on either. Initially the right-hand collar patch was to be plain black (though some members wore SS runes), but subsequently one bearing the Galician lion in white was adopted; the left-hand patch bore normal SS rank insignia. A new white-on-black outline *tryzub* collar patch motif may have been introduced to symbolize the division's change of national suffix from '*Galizische*' to '*Ukrainische*' in late 1944. Some were certainly manufactured, and despite a lack of photographic evidence some veterans apparently confirm its use in small numbers. There seems to be no suggestion that the armshield might have been changed at the same time, though this would have been logical.

The UVV were supposed to wear *Wehrmacht* uniforms without German national insignia. Instead, the cap was to display an oval yellow cockade with a blue centre (the officers' version larger and with a 'fluted' outer band); and the helmet, a diagonally halved blue-over-yellow shield. The eagle on the right breast was to be replaced by a winged swastika device, and a national armshield was to be worn on the upper right sleeve. One pattern took the form of a straight-sided shield with a white *tryzub* on a yellow-over-blue field, on a field-grey backing below the white letters 'YBB' (UVV in Cyrillic), which is consistent with the insignia prescribed for the contemporary Russian Liberation Army (ROA). Another pattern had a yellow *tryzub* on light blue with a blue 'UKRAINE' on silver across the top; it is unclear which model was the first to be introduced. The collar patches and Tsarist-style rank insignia were to be the same as for the ROA, though the latter reverted to the German pattern in March 1944. In practice, most UVV members wore a mixture of insignia (see Plate H1).

Ukrainian National Army, 1945

The Germans remained reluctant to recognize Ukraine's independence, and only did so in March 1945, when it was far too late. However, the Ukrainian National Committee had already appointed Gen Shandruk as commander of the *Ukrainska Natsionalna Armiia* (UNA), and he quickly took over.

Shandruk insisted that the 14. SS-Division should be part of this force, and it was duly transferred in April 1945, being retitled the '1st Ukrainian Division'. A 2nd Ukrainian Div was put together from some scattered UVV units including an anti-tank brigade, the 281st Reserve Inf Regt and two 'guard' regiments. During the last weeks of the war the 1st Div saw brief action in Austria, while the 2nd suffered heavy losses in Czechoslovakia. The planned integration of other UVV units was halted by the German surrender. The Ukrainians claim that the army's strength would have been 250,000, though this figure may well have included a variety of auxiliaries such as Flak Helpers. The UNA's weapons and equipment were wholly German.

*   *   *

As soon as the UNA was recognized, Shandruk set about establishing a distinctive **uniform**. For practical reasons German field-grey obviously had to be retained, but German national devices were removed (see Plate H2). Shandruk ordered that 'yellow and blue colours' should be worn on the caps and sleeves, and he and many soldiers displayed a yellow *tryzub* on a blue shield on the upper left sleeve. Shandruk himself wore a peaked cap, but other officers acquired *Mazepynka kappis* of the old *Sich* Rifles pattern.

Shandruk ordered special insignia from Prague, and by 25 April these were being worn by the 1st Div in place of the *Waffen-SS* devices. The cockade had a gold edge round a blue centre bearing a gold *tryzub*: both oval and round versions were worn. New rank devices were also introduced. According to Shandruk, these were based on designs drawn up in the 1920s, though they bore no obvious relationship to either UNR army or UHA insignia. He explains that they were placed on the shoulder straps because the corresponding Soviet devices were worn on the collar and cuffs (although in fact the Russians had re-adopted shoulder boards in 1943). Ranks were indicated by silver transverse bars with gilt German 'pips' in lieu of the traditional Ukrainian stars. A *Heneral Polkovnyk* (Gen) wore a broad bar and 3 pips; *Heneral Poruchnyk* (LtGen) and *Heneral Khorunzhyi* (MajGen), the same with 2 and 1 pips; *Polkovnyk* (Col), *Pidpolkovnyk* (LtCol) and *Maior* (Maj), a medium bar and 3, 2 and 1 pips; *Sotnyk* (Capt), *Poruchnyk* (1/Lt) and *Khorunzhyi* (2/Lt), a narrow bar with 3, 2 and 1 pips. *Bulavnyi* (SgtMaj), *Chotovyi* (Sgt), *Roiovyi* (Cpl) and *Starshyi Strilets* (L/Cpl) wore 4, 3, 2 and 1 pips. Generals wore three lines of gold cord along the front and bottom of the collar, with a loop inside the corner; field officers, two such lines; company officers, one; and NCOs, a single line without the loop.

The collar patches were shaped like those of the UNR army. In most cases the colour was the same as the shoulder strap piping, indicating arm-of-service as follows: generals and staff, crimson patch but silver strap piping; infantry, blue; artillery, red; cavalry and armour, yellow; technical troops, brown.

Lieutenant-General Pavlo Shandruk, commander-in-chief of the Ukrainian National Army sponsored by the Germans in 1945, when final defeat was only weeks away. He wears the regulation collar patches for his rank and the Simon Petlura Cross.

Waffen-Unterscharführer of the 14. Division, clearly showing the Galician lion right collar patch.

THE UKRAINIAN INSURGENT ARMY, 1941–55

Ukrainian guerrilla forces fought both Germans and Soviet occupiers in the cause of an independent Ukraine. The first insurgent units appeared in 1941, when the OUN organized three groups and sent them into the Soviet Ukraine in the wake of the advancing Germans – without the Germans' knowledge or consent, since they were opposed to nationalist activity of any kind. Unit 'North' (the largest) was aimed at Kyiv, Unit 'Centre' (the next largest) at Kharkiv, and Unit 'South' at Odesa; together they totalled some 4,000 men, and were split into *Pokhidni zvena* or marching teams of seven to ten men. Some were killed or captured by one side or the other during their advance, but others managed to get through and set up an OUN organization.

The next nationalist unit was formed a little later to fight Soviet partisan units in the Pripet Marshes: the *Poliska Sich-Ukrainska Povstanska Armiya* (UPA), Polisian *Sich*-Ukrainian Insurgent Army. In 1942 the wing of the OUN led by Stefan Bandera organized its own UPA, and the original force took the name *Ukrainska Narodno-Revoliutsiina Armiya*, Ukrainian People's Revolutionary Army; the OUN's UPA dissolved this in 1943. Since these units were fighting Soviet partisans there was a certain amount of tacit co-operation with the Germans; indeed, some members were incorporated into *Schuma* units, while others joined the 14. SS-Division in 1943. However, a substantial number remained independent, and were renamed UPA-West in December 1943.

By the end of 1942 the UPA proper had become the main resistance force, fighting both Germans and Soviet Russians alike. In late 1944 it was 20,000 to 30,000 strong, with cavalry and artillery detachments. The basic unit was the *sotnya* or company, usually operating independently, but three or four companies could be combined into a battalion for a large-scale operation. At this period the UPA was divided into three General Military Districts: 'North' (Volhynia, Zhitomir, Kyiv), 'West' (Galicia), and 'South' (Vinnitsia and Khmelnytsky); plans for an Eastern group never materialized. Each group was subdivided into districts and tactical sections.

In 1945 all Ukrainian territories came under Soviet control, and Soviet internal security forces moved in. Resistance continued until the mid-1950s, although the UPA was largely destroyed in 1948 by joint Czech, Polish and Soviet operations.

* * *

The UPA wore a variety of **uniforms**, some of them home-made and others captured German, Soviet or satellite patterns (see Plate H3). The *tryzub* was worn as a cap badge. Many of these devices were home-made, like the shield-shaped examples in the photograph of *Chotovyi* Pertsovich (see page 46), while others

Soldiers of the Ukrainian Insurgent Army (UPA), 1944. The CO of this unit (far left) wears a complete *Waffen-SS* enlisted man's uniform, while others have removed the insignia from German tunics. Civilian and Red Army garments can also be seen (e.g. second right), and a mixture of German and Soviet weapons.

were circular *Schuma*-style cockades. Functional ranks and corresponding insignia were introduced on 27 January 1944: *Holovnyi Komandyr UPA* (C-in-C), silver trident above silver oakleaves; *Kraievyi Komandyr UPA* (General Military District Cdr), red trident, red 'V'-chevron; *Komandyr Voiennoi Okruhy*, *Komandyr Zahonu* and *Komandyr Kurinnyi* (Military District, Detachment, and Battalion Cdrs), 3, 2 and 1 flat-topped 'V'-chevrons; *Sotenyi*, *Chotovyi* and *Roiovyi* (Co, Ptn and Squad Cdrs), 3, 2 and 1 red stripes. HQ personnel had yellow chevrons and were considered senior to field commanders. Insignia were worn on a black backing on the left lapel (including civilian dress) and left forearm (uniform only). The rank titles and insignia detailed on p.30 of MAA 142, *Partisan Warfare 1941–45*, seem to have been planned but not introduced. Inevitably there were local variations, and most UPA men wore no insignia at all.

The UPA used captured arms and equipment, so these would have been mainly German up to the mid-1940s. However, it also traded with the Italian, Hungarian, Rumanian and Slovak occupation troops. After 1945 most new weapons and equipment were of Soviet origin.

A record of the post-war anti-Soviet resistance: UPA soldiers photographed near Rivne, 1947. They wear a mixture of Soviet, German and Polish uniform items.

Two troopers of the UNR's 1st 'Maksym Zalizniak' Cavalry Regt, wearing uniforms of contrasting colours. Note the length of the 'shlyks' on their hats.

THE PLATES

A: WORLD WAR I

A1: Volunteer, *Legion Ukrainski Sichovi Srtiltsi* (Legion of Ukrainian *Sich* Rifles), 1914

This legionary had belonged to one of the para-military *Sichovi Striltsi* organizations. He wears his pre-war uniform, since the Legion had a low priority and regulation Austro-Hungarian uniforms and equipment were not issued until the end of the year, after the men had been fighting for three months. The only weapons provided at first were obsolete M1873 Werndl rifles without slings, so the volunteers had to make their own from string. This man has a cavalry belt and old pattern cartridge pouch.

A2: NCO, *Legion Ukrainski Sichovi Srtiltsi*, 1917

Austria-Hungary found it increasingly difficult to maintain uniform supplies as the war continued. By 1917 the situation had become so bad that the Legion's sponsors in Galicia began to supply it with its own uniform, which the Austrian authorities had no choice but to accept. This NCO wears a *Mazepinka kappi* with a blue and yellow rosette, and a tunic based on the so-called *Karlbluse*, but with distinctive pocket flaps. This supplanted the orthodox Austro-Hungarian uniform first issued at the end of 1914. A yellow-blue vertical stripe on the collar had replaced the old blue patches in 1916. (See also MAA 392, Plate G4; and MAA 397, Plate G4.)

A3: Junior officer, *Galitsko-Bukovinsky Kurin Sichovi Srtiltsi* (Galician-Bukovynian Battalion of *Sich* Rifles); Kyiv, spring 1918

Usually known as the Galician *Sich* Rifles, this elite unit was recruited from Ukrainians captured while serving in the Austro-Hungarian Army. The men wore a mixture of old Russian, old Austro-Hungarian and new Ukrainian uniforms,

the former being the commonest. In the Central *Rada* period the main distinction consisted of the blue patches on the greatcoat collar. These *Sichovi Srtiltsi* wore these with yellow Cyrillic letters 'CC' (SS) superimposed. Some officers also had such patches on their jackets. The blue armband was the insignia of the Kyiv garrison (because it was formed there, this unit was sometimes known as the Kyiv *Sich* Rifles). The looped silver chevron on the right sleeve is the rank insignia. The cap bears the St Mikhail cockade described in the body text. The Nagant revolver holster is carried on a private's belt.

B: THE UNR
B1: Volunteer, *Kurin Chervonyh Haidamakiv* (Battalion of Red Haidamaks) of the *Haidamatsky Kish Slobidskoy Ukrainy* (Haidamak Host of North-Eastern Ukraine); winter 1918
Although red later became synonymous with the Bolsheviks, most of the left-leaning Ukrainian political parties used it at this period. The uniform worn by this volunteer combines it with 'national' elements. The traditional *koochma* or fur hat has a long *shlyk* or cloth tail decorated with gold lace and tassel. He has shaved his head in the old Ukrainian Cossack fashion, leaving only a tuft on the crown. His sheepskin *kozhukh* has been dressed to give it a red colour. After the troops returned to Kyiv with the Germans the *kozhukhs* were replaced by army greatcoats. The *sharovary* or Cossack trousers were made from regulation khaki cloth. Although ankle boots with puttees were worn, the traditional high boots were found to be much better during cold and muddy weather. The regulation bread bag was usually used to carry extra ammunition. The Black *Haidamaks* (*Kurin Chornyh Haidamakiv*) who formed the second part of this Host – raised mostly from Kyiv students and schoolboys – had black *shlyks* and wore greatcoats from the outset.

B2: Soldier, Ivan Bogun Regiment, winter 1918
This unit was raised in October 1917 as Kyiv's representative of the Regiment of Knights of St George, composed of recipients of Imperial Russia's highest military award. After independence it was renamed after one of the Cossack leaders during Bogdan Khmelnitsky's 17th century uprising against Polish rule. Most of its officers disagreed with the concept of a separate Ukrainian Army and left in late autumn 1917, while the men chose to hang out white flags during the fighting with the Bolsheviks in January 1918. This soldier has removed his cockade in order to indicate his neutrality. He is dressed according to the height of military fashion at the time, with the crown of his cap pulled down at the sides and his blouse shortened. The orange piping on cuffs and breeches and the orange and black striped ribbon on the chest of the blouse were St George's unit distinctions, but the shoulder straps have been removed; many soldiers disliked these reminders of the Tsarist

Polkovnyk (Col) Gnat Stefaniv of the Western Ukrainian UHA, 1919. The field officers' *zubchatka* – zig-zag collar patch – and sleeve insignia of the April 1919 regulations can be seen clearly.

regime and did not obey the January 1918 order introducing new blue straps piped with yellow. (The original shoulder strap is shown in MAA 364, *The Russian Army 1914–18*, Plate H7.)

B3: Private, 1st *Persha Ukrainska* ('*Sinyozhupanna*') *Dyviziya* (1st Ukrainian 'Bluecoat' Division), March 1918
The 1st 'Bluecoat' Div arrived in Kyiv in March 1918. Its role had been envisaged as internal security rather than combat, so its uniform was more 'national' than military, based on traditional Ukrainian peasant dress with some Cossack features. The long-skirted *zhupan* (coat) had three to five large pleats in the back. The 1st Div had a small *shlyk* secured by a large blue-yellow rosette on its fur hat; the 2nd did not. This *shlyk* was usually worn hanging to the front, but for some unknown reason it was turned to the left during the first parade. The Germans gave the 1st Div captured Russian weapons but German personal equipment, which was changed to the Russian pattern immediately after its arrival in Kyiv.

C: THE HETMANATE
C1: Captain, 1st *Serdiuk* (Guards) Infantry Regiment, 1918
This was the only force the Germans let the Hetman raise other than security troops and a personal escort. Although its officers and men were selected from the more conservative elements, they did not fight well during the anti-Hetmanate uprising, and most eventually joined the Directory. Only the cavalry received a new dress uniform (similar to that of the Imperial Russian Hussars but in blue and yellow), so most of the others wore standard Russian Army field dress – here the so-called 'French' – with new shoulder straps and cockades. Some officers wore the new coloured peaked caps and took advantage of a provision allowing them to have darker cuffs and collars (in this case, made from field-grey material). The breeches stripes were unique to this division. When the Hetman's opponents adopted red rosettes in late 1918, those who remained loyal to him chose white ones (often placed behind their cap cockades, as here). The equipment is of the 1912 Russian pattern.

C2: *Hetman* Pavlo Skoropadski, 1918
Pavlo Skoropadsky was a descendent of Ivan Skoropadski, the Hetman (the old title for a Cossack leader in Ukraine) between 1708 and 1722. Although he introduced a Cossack-style uniform into the army, he never adopted it himself (nor the service dress generally worn by those who had served in the old Imperial Russian Army). Instead, he wore a black uniform cut along Caucasian Cossack lines, or else a white version. He has a Caucasian sabre and dagger and carries a miniature mace, an old Ukrainian symbol of command. As a rule the only decoration he wore was the cross of the Order of St George (4th Class) which he had been awarded for fighting the Germans in August 1914; however, Kaiser Wilhelm II honoured him with the Order of

Colonel Mikhail Koshchuk, CO of the 4th Regt, 1st Division, Ukrainian National Army (UNA) – the former 14. SS-Division. Note the piped *Mazepynka kappi* with oval cockade, the new rank insignia (three 'pips' and a medium band), and the absence of collar patches.

the Red Eagle (1st Class) during his visit to Germany, and this is shown on his breast.

C3: *Znachkovyi Hetmana Ukrajiny* (personal ADC to the Hetman of Ukraine), 1918

Although *Hetman* Skoropadski favoured eventual federation with White Russia, he tried to develop a distinctively national style of uniform. During the summer of 1918 his HQ, Personal Escort, *Serdiuk* (Guard) units and all generals received a new uniform based on the *zhupan* coat in a pseudo-Cossack style. The Hetman's aides wore trefoils on the ends of the chest braids and on the crown of the hat. Note the crossed maces badge above the cap cockade, and aiguillettes as worn by ADCs in the old Russian Army. This *Znachkovyi* also wears the Escort's cipher and brick-red piping on his gold-laced shoulder straps, together

with the Order of St Vladimir (4th Class, with Swords), and the badge for graduates of the General Staff Academy, all from the old Imperial Russian Army. Small gold slides on the chin strap were a *Serdiuk* Division distinction. He wears general officers' *sharovary* instead of the regulation breeches.

D: THE DIRECTORY

D1: Major, HQ *Persha Kozatstko-Striletska (Sirozhupanna) Dyvizia* (1st Cossack Rifle 'Greycoat' Division), 1918–19

The division's uniform was an interesting attempt to combine old Cossack traditions with modern field dress, and provided the model for the Directory's subsequent attempt to do the same. The distinctive grey material was actually poor quality undyed Austrian woollen cloth.

The division had its own rank insignia in the form of horizontal wheat-ears in gilt worn on the collar – initially with a blue and yellow stripe behind and later, after its transfer to Ukraine, on collar patches: crimson, as here, for divisional HQ personnel, medics, officials and priests, green for infantry, red for artillery and black for engineers. The red rosette under the cap cockade was worn by all the Directory troops in late 1918 to early 1919. The white armband was worn in January 1919 during a night attack on the town of Ovruch, which had been captured by the Reds. The 'Greycoats' continued to fight with the Directory forces until the end of 1920, the survivors eventually being interned in Poland, though there is little evidence of their distinctive uniforms after mid-1919.

D2: *Otaman* (Commander) of Guerrilla Detachment Bojko, 1919

The Directory's attempt to introduce a new uniform based on traditional Cossack dress failed through lack of time and resources, but some units did try to dress in the preferred style. They were mostly cavalry or guerrilla groups, and the actual details generally depended on availability and individual taste. The most elaborate outfits were worn by the commanders of the various semi-independent guerrilla detachments like *Otaman* Bojko, the commander of the '*orijska Sich*' (later the 2nd Div in the UNR army). In order to look like an authentic Cossack leader he even broke into a museum and took an old Cossack colonel's mace and 17th century sabre... In the summer of 1919 the self-willed Bojko was arrested and his division disbanded.

RANK INSIGNIA

(First row) Central *Rada*, December 1917: *Otaman Armii* (army commander); *Otaman Brigady* (brigade commander); *Sotnyk* (company commander); *Chotar* (platoon sergeant).
(Second row) Hetmanate, June 1918: *Heneralnyi Znachkovyi* (lieutenant-general); *Vijskovyi Starshina* (lieutenant-colonel); *Znachkovyi* (lieutenant); conscript *Roiovyi* (corporal).
(Third row) UNR, April 1919: *Otaman* (general), *Osavul* (lieutenant-colonel); *Chotar* (lieutenant); *Roiovyi* (corporal).
(Fourth row) UHA, April 1919: *Heneral Poruchnyk* (lieutenant-general); *Pidpolkovnyk* (lieutenant-colonel); *Poruchnik* (first lieutenant); *Vistun* (corporal).
(Bottom row) UNR, April 1920: *Heneral Poruchnyk* (lieutenant-general); *Pidpolkovnyk* (lieutenant-colonel); *Sotnyk* (captain); *Roiovyi* (corporal).
(Drawing by Dmitro Adamenko)

D3: Private, *Chorni Zaporizhski* (Black Zaporozhian) cavalry regiment, 1919

This colourful unit was formed in 1917 and distinguished itself as much by its recklessness as its courage. It provoked the clash with Denikin's White troops in Kyiv in August 1919, which resulted in the expulsion of the Directory troops. During the winter of 1917–18 the *Chornoshlychniki* ('Black Shlyks') wore a black or grey Cossack uniform and small fur hats with exaggeratedly long black *shlyks*. During the Hetmanate period they wore standard cavalry uniforms, but during the winter of 1918–19 after the fall of the Hetman they succeeded in obtaining supplies of black and light grey cloth and reverted to their old uniforms. Unfortunately, there was no way to replenish these, so by the end of the year they (like most Ukrainian units) were in rags. This trooper is armed with the M1881/1909 Cossack *shashka* sabre and cavalry revolver.

E1: General Staff officer, 1919

In spring 1919 the Directory was forced to recognize that its Cossack-style uniform was too impracticable for field wear and too expensive for mass production. As a result a new uniform resembling the April 1918 pattern was introduced. Arm-of-service was to be shown by the colour of the peaked cap band, collar patches, and cloth triangles above the cuffs; rank insignia took the form of looped chevrons worn above the triangles. In practice even this simplified uniform was found to be too elaborate for an army which was constantly in a life-and-death struggle, and as a result most soldiers and many junior officers had no insignia at all. To remedy this, a large cloth trident in the arm or service colour (here, black piped with white) was added to the upper left sleeve in July 1919.

E2: *Holovnyi Otaman* (Commander-in-Chief) Simon Petlura, 1919

Petlura wears the regulation field uniform introduced in April 1919, with the simplified insignia decreed in July. His rank insignia are placed directly on the plain collar; generals wore it on both sides, and all more junior ranks on the right with an arm-of-service device on the left. A large *tryzub* in arm-of-service colour was worn on the left sleeve; no colour was prescribed for generals, but most wore it in gold, as Petlura does here.

E3: Officer, 1st *Gutusul* Marine Regiment, 1919

The creation of this regiment in spring 1919 was one of the few successes of the military co-operation between the UNR and the ZUNR. It was formed by the UNR, but most of the men were *Gutusuls* (Ukrainians living in the Carpathians) from the ZUNR. A 2nd Marine Regt was raised in summer 1919 from UNR nationals. By the end of 1920 both had been combined and reduced to a single company. The 1st Regt wore this stylish black uniform with crimson and gold insignia, but the 2nd had to wear Russian naval uniforms. Other ranks of the 1st Regt wore a sailor's hat with the regimental title in gold letters on the black ribbon. Although a UNR unit, the Marines wore UHA rank insignia; note the three gold cuff bands terminating in rosettes.

F: THE ZUNR

F1: Cavalryman, 1st Brigade, UHA, 1919

The Austro-Hungarian Ukrainian Legion's few cavalrymen were used as HQ guards and messengers. Even though the UHA inherited a number of Ukrainian troopers from the old Austrian cavalry regiments, it was unable to create a strong cavalry force; it raised one cavalry brigade of two regiments together with an independent regiment, but these never played a significant role in combat. Ex-Legion troopers tried to keep their old uniform (including the Austro-Hungarian cavalry pelisse), but added the new UHA insignia. The red *zubchatka* or zig-zag collar patch was non-regulation.

F2: Lieutenant-colonel, UHA cavalry, 1919

The UHA uniform regulated in April 1919 used grey-green material from old Austro-Hungarian stocks. Although certain units continued to wear the old Ukrainian *Sich* Rifles' *Mazepinska kappi*, most had the peaked cap as shown here. Apart from the cuff rank insignia, the most distinctive element was the *zubchatka*, in this case in the cavalry's regulation yellow. This patch was to remain a characteristic feature of uniforms worn by Ukrainian units during World War II. The sabre is the M1904 Austro-Hungarian model with Kaiser Karl's monogram still on its sword-knot. (See also MAA 305, *The Russian Civil War (2): White Armies*, Plate C3; note, however, that the blue crown on that figure's *kappi* is incorrect.)

F3: *Bulavny Desiatnik* of the *Narodna Storoja* (People's Guard), ZUNR, 1919

After five years of war there were a great many deserters, refugees and ex-POWs at large in the countryside. To counter them, a People's Guard was raised from local volunteers, many of them former Austrian Gendarmes. The Guard had no official uniform or insignia until August 1919, when specific headdress, collar patches and insignia were introduced. This senior NCO still wears the old Austrian Gendarmerie coat with long-service chevrons, but has added new Ukrainian insignia. The awards are also from the old regime: the 1908 Jubilee Cross for Civil Service, and the Good Service Badge 2nd Class for rank and file. He is armed with the Mannlicher M1895 Gendarmerie carbine and the Gendarmerie pattern sabre for senior NCOs.

G: WORLD WAR II

G1: Junior officer, *Karpatska Sich* (Carpathian Sich), 1939

This para-military organization was called upon in March 1939 to defend the tiny newborn state of Carpatho-Ukraine. The

A platoon commander of the Insurgent Army: UPA *Chotovyi* Ivan Pertsovich (aka 'Lisovik'). Note the shield-shaped *kappi* badge with *tryzub* motif.

...p of re-enactors in authentic uniforms of the ...ian Insurgent Army. The crouching figure at left ...a Police uniform modified along UPA lines, with ...epynka band to the cap and a blue-and-yellow sleeve ...l; the second wears *Generalgouvernement* Police ...rm; the standing figure at left wears one of the many ...nt *Schuma* outfits, with yellow-over-blue swallow-tail ...nants on the collar; the centre man, a light grey ...ssibly home-made) UPA tunic; and the third, a green ...rainian Land Service tunic with 'LANDDIENST UKRAINA' ...ff title.

...rey-green colour had been worn by the UHA: it may also ...ave been chosen because the *Sich's* Czech and Hungarian ...pponents both wore khaki. On parade officers wore this ...niform with a white shirt and dark tie. The men had puttees ...stead of field boots, and plain belts. The only insignia worn ...y this appointee is a yellow-over-blue ribbon in the 'V'-...naped cut-out of his *kappi*. The volunteers had Czech ...quipment and small arms.

2: Officer, 'Roland' Battalion, 1941

...he two battalion-sized Ukrainian units which accompanied ...e German forces into the Soviet-occupied Ukraine were ...nown officially as Special Group *Nachtigall* ('Nightingale') ...nd Organization *Roland*. Both were short-lived, being ...sbanded by the end of 1941. *Nachtigall* wore German ...rmy uniforms without special insignia other than the small ...ue-yellow loops worn by some on the shoulder straps, but ...oland had its own uniform. This was modified from old ...zechoslovak Army issue, but with shoulder straps replaced ...ith a single shoulder cord; a crimson UHA-pattern ...ubchatka on the collar; specially designed rank insignia on ...e cuffs; a Ukrainian cockade with *tryzub* on the field cap, ...nd a yellow brassard with '*Deutsche Wehrmacht*' in black.

3: NCO of a Ukrainian Security Battalion, ...1942

...July 1941 the German *Ordnungspolizei* (Order Police) in ...e occupied Eastern Territories began organizing municipal ...rmations called *Schutzmannschaftsbataillonen* (Guard ...attalions) in Ukraine. These *Schuma* units wore a variety of ...niforms ranging from ex-Soviet Army to black *Algemeine-*...S, while some even managed to create their own uniforms ...nd rank insignia. These early outfits proved to be ...npractical for combat operations and were gradually ...eplaced with standard *Polizei* green or even *Wehrmacht* ...eld-grey uniforms, often with some kind of Ukrainian ...signia – e.g. the crimson *zubchatka* worn here on the collar ...f his *Polizei* tunic. (See also MAA 142, *Partisan Warfare* ...941–45, Plates B2 & B3.)

: WORLD WAR II & AFTER

1: Private, *Ukrainske Vizvolne Vijsko* ...Jkrainian Liberation Army), 1943–44

...he UVV was created in 1943 as an umbrella organization for ...l the Ukrainian units scattered throughout the *Wehrmacht*. ...theory their uniform was to be that of the German Army's ...*sttruppen*, with the same Tsarist-style rank insignia as the ...ussian Liberation Army, a 'national' cockade and ...rmshield. The latter was in the UNR's original colours of ...ellow-over-blue rather than the later blue-over-yellow, and ...ore a white outline trident and the Cyrillic letters YBB

('UVV'). UVV soldiers were supposed to remove the eagle and swastika insignia from their German caps and tunics, but in practice few did.

H2: Major, *Ukrainska Natsionalna Armija* (Ukrainian National Army), 1945

It was only in March 1945 that the Third Reich agreed to recognize the Ukrainian National Committee and create a Ukrainian National Army. A new uniform was quickly designed, but only a few officers managed to obtain it before the war ended. However, the rest of the troops adopted it in the Allied prison camps. It was necessarily based on the German uniform, but with Ukrainian cockades, shoulder straps and collar patches. This former member of the 14th SS-Division '*Galizien*' has the new cockade and rank insignia. He has removed the SS collar patches and sleeve eagle, but retains the Galician armshield. He has also cut out the silver Galician lion from his collar patch and added it to the right side of his cap.

H3: Commander, *Ukrainska Povstanska Armija* (Ukrainian Insurgent Army), 1949

The first Ukrainian nationalist guerrilla detachments had no official uniform, but most of their members adopted some form of national insignia, such as yellow-blue or blue-yellow brassards, patches or hand-made trident badges. The UPA created by the Revolutionary OUN in early 1943 had no official uniform either, though some projects existed. Its members usually wore a mixture of civilian clothes and German or Soviet items. Hungarian, Italian and Slovak uniform items were also worn, with Czech and Polish ones after 1945. As the UPA expanded, it developed its own supply system to provide various necessities, including uniforms. The latter were usually made of grey homespun by local tailors. This commander wears a typical mixture: a cap modified along *Mazepynka* lines (popular among UPA personnel), a *Waffen-SS* tunic with the insignia removed, and Soviet breeches. He wears a breast badge commemo-rating the *Roland* and *Nachtigall* units, and carries a PPSh-41 SMG, a P08 pistol and German grenades.

INDEX